THE CONTROL FREAK

RESOURCES BY DR. LES PARROTT

BOOKS
High-Maintenance Relationships
Love's Unseen Enemy
Helping the Struggling Adolescent
7 Secrets of a Healthy Dating Relationship
Once upon a Family
Counseling and Psychotherapy

BOOKS WRITTEN BY DR. LES PARROTT AND DR. LESLIE PARROTT
Relationships
A Good Friend
Becoming Soul Mates
Proverbs for Couples
The Marriage Mentor Manual
Love Is
Questions Couples Ask
Getting Ready for the Wedding
Saving Your Marriage Before It Starts

VIDEO CURRICULUM
Mentoring Engaged and Newlywed Couples
Saving Your Marriage Before It Starts
Relationships

BOOKS ON TAPE
Saving Your Marriage Before It Starts
Relationships

Resources available at **www.RealRelationships.com**

THE
CONTROL
FREAK

Tyndale House Publishers Wheaton, Illinois

LES PARROTT III, Ph.D.

Visit Tyndale's exciting Web site at www.tyndale.com

The Control Freak
Copyright © 2000 by Les Parrott III. All rights reserved.

Designed by Jackie Noe

Edited by Lynn Vanderzalm

Library of Congress Cataloging-in-Publication Data

Parrott, Les.
   The control freak / Les Parrott III.
      p. cm.
   Includes bibliographical references.
   ISBN 0-8423-3792-X (hardcover)—ISBN 0-8423-3793-8 (pbk.)
   1. Control (Psychology)   I. Title.

BF611 .P37 2000
158.2—dc21   00-022191

Printed in the United States of America

06   05   04   03   02
8   7   6   5   4   3

CONTENTS

ACKNOWLEDGMENTS

Thanks . . .

To Ron Beers, Ken Petersen, Dan Balow, Travis Thrasher, and all of the other Tyndale House people who gave enthusiastic support to this project. Your collective character and good-hearted manner make working with you a true pleasure.

To my research assistant, Chris Fick, who spent countless hours in endless stacks of numerous libraries retrieving a wide variety of resources for me. Your skill and efficiency are unparalleled in my experience.

To my administrative assistant, Mindy Galbreath, who consistently goes the extra mile to keep my life running in order. Your positive spirit and dedication to Leslie and me are true gifts.

To my publicist, Janice Lundquist, who, after years of working together, continues to amaze me with her professional savvy. Your expert skill and kind friendship have become indispensable.

To my editor, Lynn Vanderzalm, who allowed a Control Freak author to interrupt more than one salmon dinner for the sake of this book. Your giftedness as an editor and your quality as a person gently and almost painlessly guided me through every review, revision, and rewrite.

To my wife, Leslie, who dreams my dreams, empowers my spirit, and fills my days with unimaginable love. Your charm and winsome ways are too often taken for granted by me, but I couldn't survive a day without them.

To my unfailing God, who accepts this woeful soul trying too often to control things far beyond his reach. Your grace sustains me.

CONFESSIONS OF A CONTROL FREAK

If you read this book, take my self-tests, and make sure to follow my advice exactly as I tell you . . .

Let me rephrase that.

I'm the first to admit I have controlling tendencies. I can be prescriptive, opinionated, impatient, and tenacious. I don't have difficulty asserting myself and making my own needs known. In my drive to get the job done, I can be insensitive to other people's feelings. Most of the time I keep these tendencies in check, but if I'm under pressure and overscheduled, my dictatorial side is likely to leak out. But am I a certifiable Control Freak? That's a matter of opinion. Namely, my wife's.

When I first told Leslie I was going to write a book called *The Control Freak*, she quickly quipped: "Oh, you're finally writing your autobiography?" We both laughed. But I'm smart enough to know her tease revealed some truth. And it would be sanctimonious of me to begin this book without owning up to my tendency to take charge. I'm not talking about taking charge of the TV remote—that's a given. What guy can't be accused of being a clickaholic? And I'm not talking about the extreme compulsion to control everyone else's daily diet and behavior. But when it comes to things that matter most to me, I like to run the show. And depending on the time and place, my controlling tendencies can concern anything from choosing a restaurant (not to mention the table) to deciding how to structure a budget. Most of all, I'm supercontrolling of my personal schedule. I don't hyperventilate if I don't get to set my own itinerary, but I do my best to protect how I use my own time.

You probably picked up this book because you are trying to cope with a Control Freak in your life—don't fear, the bulk of this book is devoted to helping you do just that. But, at the outset, I believe it is helpful to own up to any controlling tendencies you might have. Why? To be honest, all of us are a little controlling at times. Don't you sometimes become irritable if things aren't done just the way you want them? Don't you sometimes become a little too rigid or demanding? It's only human. And it's safe to say that almost everyone is a Control Freak some of the time, which leads me to a definition:

Control Freaks are people who care more than you do about something and won't stop at being pushy to get their way.

Take sports, as a potentially innocuous example. If someone cares more about watching *Monday Night Football* than you do, chances are he will not only reserve the best TV in the house when the games are broadcast but also schedule his day—or even the family vacation—around it. You know better than to interfere with that person's desire to watch those games. The football fan is in control. Now, this fan may not be a Control Freak all the time in every situation, but on Monday night, watch out! And that may be okay with you as long as it doesn't interfere with your Monday-night plans. But what happens if you wanted to have a book-club meeting, and because of schedules the only night that works coincides with a Monday night when the fan is hogging the TV room and won't budge? "Give me a break," you might say to the fan. "You always get the TV, and just this once I'm asking you to watch your game somewhere else." If the fan refuses—presto—he is suddenly a pushy Control Freak. Am I right?

The point is that Control Freaks are people who care about something—anything—more than you do. It may be the way they like their scrambled eggs prepared, the way they answer their phone at work, the way the car is parked in the garage, or anything else you can imagine. Not only do they care about something more than you do, they become downright pushy to make sure the thing they care about is done the way they want it done. That's why everybody is a Control Freak some of the time.

By the way, calling someone a Control Freak is not necessarily disparaging. Sure, Control Freaks can be pushy, self-centered cranks who always have to have their own way. They can be the proverbial bull in a china shop. They can be the power-hungry boss who tells you what your opinion is supposed to be. Or the manipulative mother who bombards you with criticisms and prophecies of doom until you do what she wants. These are major-league Control Freaks, and there's no ambivalence about the trouble they cause.

But a Control Freak can also be anyone who cares more about how to clean the kitchen than you do or how to schedule a meeting or what color the couch in the living room should be. You see, the term *Control Freak* is not so much derogatory as it is descriptive. So, relax. And maybe admit—along with me—that you can be a Control Freak. As we will see, recognizing the Control Freak in yourself will help you more successfully manage the Control Freaks around you.

GETTING THE MOST FROM THIS BOOK

I have two goals in writing this book: to help you cope with the Control Freaks in your life and to help you control the Control Freak inside you. Part 1—"Who's in Control?"—discusses the positive and negative aspects of several major control issues. Chapter 2 gives you tools for recognizing Control Freaks and a self-test for determining how controlling the Control Freaks in your life really are. Chapter 3 examines the anatomy of a Control Freak, revealing the top ten qualities Control Freaks have in common. Chapter 4 asks an important question: Is all control bad? Though people's overcontrolling tendencies can drive us crazy, we can't afford to throw the Control Freak out with the proverbial bathwater. I close part 1 of the book with a discussion about why some people have such a compulsion to control. This is a crucial question for anyone wanting to find peace with a controlling boss, parent, spouse, or whomever.

Part 2 explores ways of coping with the Control Freaks around us. Here, we take a serious look at the Control Freaks we sometimes work for and work with as well as the Control Freaks closer to home, those who may have raised us or whom we may be raising. Of course, we will also explore the Control Freaks you are related to by marriage, whether they are your spouse or your in-laws. Regardless of where you seem to encounter your most troublesome controller, you will find a toolbox of trade secrets for making that relationship better. I'll help you pinpoint the trouble spots with a specific person in your life, show you why he or she is so overly controlling and, most important, what you can do right now to make your relationship with that person better or at least come to a place in which you can find peace and joy in spite of the controlling ways. It's a tall order, but I've worked with enough people in predicaments that are probably pretty similar to yours to know you can do a good job of coping with the Control Freaks around you.

Part 3 just may be the most helpful for some of you. Here the focus is on controlling the Control Freak within. I will help you diagnose your own Control Freak symptoms and reveal their primary causes. I'll also pose some questions that may uncover more about your compulsion to control than you wanted to know. But your honest answers will provide the prescription for becoming the person you long to be. In this section of the book I'll also help you rebuild and repair the relationships that may have suffered as a result of your compulsion for control. I'll show you how to set up safeguards to keep your controlling tendencies in check. Another chapter gives a three-point plan that has proved successful with countless other people in your shoes. The final chapter will show you how to maintain your influence without

being obnoxious. This is also where you will find the "transforming truth" that every recovering Control Freak needs to learn.

I hope and pray that your journey through these pages is time well
spent. If you're like me, you can't afford to spend time reading a
book that doesn't deliver what it claims. I've done my best to
insure that doesn't happen. Ultimately, you will be the one who
knows for sure. And ultimately, you—with God's grace—will be
the one who deals effectively with the Control Freaks around you
and who controls the Control Freak in yourself. I wish you every
success in doing so.

PART 1

WHO'S IN CONTROL?

2

EXPOSING THE CONTROL FREAK

*Control: To exercise authoritative or dominating influence over; to hold
in restraint; to regulate, to influence, to master, to restrain.*

THE AMERICAN HERITAGE DICTIONARY OF THE ENGLISH LANGUAGE

I was about to appear on a television talk show in New York to
discuss my book *High-Maintenance Relationships* when the
producer walked into the greenroom and shook my hand. "I love
your book," she said, "but I need more than a chapter on the
Control Freak." She went on to describe how her job required her
to be in control of controlling people.

A few minutes later a well-known celebrity walked into the
room. "Where are the muffins?" he demanded. "Can somebody
get me a pastry?" His publicist scurried to meet his needs. "I'll be
on for two segments, right?" he asked the producer.

She looked at me and raised her eyebrows, as if to say, "See
what I mean?"

▼▼▼

I was in the middle of a premarital counseling session with two
very in-love people. We were reviewing the results of a compatibil-
ity test when a woman ignored the Privacy sign, knocked on the
door, and stuck her head in the office: "Oh, I thought you two
might be in here, and I wanted to let you know your father and I
are going to take you to dinner when you're done with the counselor." It was the groom's mother. "We'll be out in the car when

you're ready," she continued, "but take your time—five or ten minutes maybe?"

The young man wilted and started to put on his coat to leave. His fiancée was shocked not only by her soon-to-be mother-in-law's intrusiveness but also by her soon-to-be-husband's compliance. "What are you doing?" she asked him. The three of us spent the remaining thirty minutes of our session talking about controlling parents—and in-laws.

▼▼▼

When a friend of mine learned I was writing a book about Control Freaks, she immediately blurted out, "Oh, you've got to write a chapter about my boss. He is the most opinionated and demanding man I've ever met." She went on to tell me that no matter how convincing someone else's ideas are, he always insists on doing things his way—even if it is more expensive or unnecessary. She also told me it was nearly impossible for this man to delegate. Her boss leaves nothing to chance. He is known for his "just checking" calls to be sure his employees are doing what he wants, the way he wants. Only he knows how things should really be done. "Whatever job he gives you," she told me, "you can be certain he will eventually critique it, amend it, correct it, improve on it, upgrade it, or in some other way put his stamp on it."

> "Kindly let me help you or you will drown," said the monkey, putting the fish safely up in a tree.
>
> ALAN WATTS

▼▼▼

So many people I talk to—from pastors to pilots, from sales clerks to spouses—know people who have adopted Frank Sinatra's "My Way" as their personal anthem. Unfortunately, these Control Freaks have adjusted the lyrics a bit. Not only do they sing "I did it my way," but they also add, "and you'll learn to do it my way too."

At any given moment, millions of Americans are scrambling to take control of their jobs, spouses, kids, health, and time. And it seems nothing is too petty to dismiss as an opportunity to prove they are living life *their* way, making life an exhausting war of wills for everyone they encounter.

The battle for control can happen between two strangers—silently fighting over who gets the armrest on a crowded airplane. Or the battle can ignite between a loving husband and wife, each of whom is trying to convince the other that his or her choice for the evening's video rental is best. With Control Freaks any and every situation can become a competition for control. The struggle may be over a parking space, the room temperature, or whether you should use plastic wrap or Tupperware to save the leftover tuna salad. Most Control Freaks will do just about anything to get their own way.

> Who controls the past, controls the future; who controls the present, controls the past.
>
> GEORGE ORWELL

THE "MY WAY" HIGHWAY IS A LONELY ROAD

Have you ever felt forced to do something that someone else wanted you to do? Or maybe you've felt pressure to become the kind of person someone else wanted you to be.

Psychologists have described the source of that pressure in a variety of ways: a "will to conquer," an "instinct to master," a "manipulative drive," a "striving for superiority," and an "urge toward competence." It doesn't really matter what you call it; if you've ever been repeatedly roped into somebody else's ways of doing and being, you know what it feels like to be had by a Control Freak.

> You have no idea how promising the world begins to look once you have decided to have it all for yourself.
>
> ANITA BROOKNER

And that's why everyone who has ever been in the presence of a bona fide Control Freak knows the feeling—not only of being annoyed but also of being demeaned. Those are natural by-products of the Control Freak in action. The very act of someone's trying to control you sends several negative messages: I don't trust you to be able to do it right; I don't respect your judgment; I don't think you are competent; I don't value your insight (or skill or experience). Isn't it true? You feel disrespected because the Control Freak seems to assume you know nothing. Control Freaks can rob you of your sense of confidence and self-control.

Just how does that happen? Control Freaks' techniques are numerous: showing false friendliness, giving expensive gifts, making empty promises, sulking, shouting, nagging, being chronically late, withholding affection, bullying, badgering, or just plain bossing the people around them. The tools of the control trade are infinite.

> God asks no one whether he will accept life. This is not the choice. The only choice you have as you go through life is how you will live it.
>
> BERNARD MELTZER

For Control Freaks, everything has to be just so. But why? Why can't they live and let live? More important, why do we allow ourselves to be controlled by them? We'll get to these questions and many others in later chapters. We begin, however, by assessing the situation. Your situation. Just how much control do the Control Freaks around you have?

Do you know someone who flips out if you spill something on the floor? Do you know someone who takes credit for your successes? Do you know people who lose it because one of their pens is missing from the pen jar on their desk? Do you know people who know exactly how everything should be done and have no problem telling you? Do you know someone who invades your privacy? Do you know people who are so organized they would heckle Martha Stewart for being sloppy?

If you answered yes to more than one of these questions, that's a pretty good sign you know a Control Freak. But the following self-test will help you assess just how controlling that Control Freak is.

THE CONTROL FREAK SELF-TEST

Take a moment to answer these twenty-five questions as honestly as you can by circling either *Y* for yes or *N* for no.

Y   N   **1.** When I hear the words *Control Freak,* I can immediately identify a person in my life.

Y   N   **2.** When I hear the words *Control Freak,* I have *more* than one person who comes to mind. (If you think of more than one person, do the test for each one.)

Y   N   **3.** Most other people, not just me, would describe this person as picky, critical, or controlling.

Y   N   **4.** I find myself doing things I would never do if I did not feel pressured by this controlling person.

Y   N   **5.** This person would rather give orders than take them.

Y   N   **6.** This person's day is ruined if you sit on his or her perfectly made bed or do something similar to mess up his or her neatly ordered world.

Y   N   **7.** I sometimes feel used by this person.

Y   N   **8.** This person hangs on to a project forever because he or she wants it to be perfect.

Y   N   **9.** This person loves order (don't even think about touching things on his or her desk) and established routines (watch out if his or her plans have to be rearranged).

Y   N   **10.** This person's controlling tendencies cause people to feel anxious, if not alienated.

Y   N   **11.** On more than one occasion I have felt that this person was snooping around where he or she didn't belong.

Y   N   **12.** This person feels most comfortable when he or she is in charge.

Y   N   **13.** Like a bulldog, this person holds on to the way he or she wants things done.

Y   N   **14.** This person can be indecisive because he or she continues to mull over an idea and puts everything else on hold.

Y   N   **15.** If something isn't exactly to this person's liking, he or she reflexively points it out—even at the risk of embarrassing others.

Y   N   **16.** Most people, at least at first, are surprised by this person's demanding style.

Y   N   **17.** This person has his or her way of doing things and almost never budges.

Y   N   **18.** Hardly anyone would describe this person as flexible and easygoing.

Y   N   **19.** If this person does give in to another's idea, he or she doesn't fully jump onboard with it.

Y   N   **20.** If there is the slightest thing out of place, this person will find it.

Y   N   **21.** Once this person decides on something, it is settled; all other options cease to exist.

Y   N   **22.** It seems that winning an argument is more important to this person than finding the best solution.

Y   N   **23.** If this person doesn't get what he or she wants, you can count on a good display of anger, pouting, or the silent treatment.

Y   N   **24.** While driving a car, this person would rather get lost than ask for directions.

Y   N   **25.** Most people end up doing what this person wants.

SCORING

To find your test score, add the number of yes answers and multiply by four:

Total yes answers _____ x 4 = score _____. A total score of 100 is possible, and the scale that follows will help you interpret your results.

0–24   Count your blessings. Relative to most other people, you have very few, if any, controlling people in your life. On second thought, this also raises a caution flag. Perhaps you don't see other people as controlling because *you* are controlling the people around you. What do you think? I suggest you muster up your courage and ask two or three people who know you well and whose opinions you trust if they ever see you as controlling. If they do, you will want to pay special attention to part 3 of this book.

25–49   You know what it's like to be with a Control Freak, but you're certainly not in the worst of situations. You probably have a few isolated incidents of finding yourself with someone who is argumentative, nitpicky, invasive, or obnoxious. Fortunately, this person is not consistently controlling, or at least you don't have to deal with him or her on a regular basis. Still, you can benefit from some fresh approaches to making your interactions with controlling people better.

50–74   You have your work cut out for you. Whether the Control Freak in your life is found at work, at home, or somewhere else, you are going to need every tool you can find to regain some of the control you have lost to this person. With the help of this book, you will also want to take a good look at what you are doing to allow another person to gain so much control over you and your life.

75–100   Unfortunately, you are up against a full-throttle, no-holds-barred Control Freak. You are dealing with someone whose craving for control is never satisfied. As a result, you are going to need to give yourself fully to finding new ways of coping with this person—and changing the way you interact with him or her. Give yourself ample time to study and reflect on the personalized strategy you will design as a result of your reading. You may even want to augment your reading with a session or two from a support group or a counselor who can coach you through this important process.

YOU DON'T HAVE TO BE CONTROLLED

Whatever your score on the preceding self-test, you have good reason to be hopeful. After many months of gathering the latest and most reliable studies on coping with Control Freaks, I'm optimistic about your ability to make significant progress with even the most die-hard control addicts. It boils down to understanding your choices.

> No man need stay the way he is.
>
> HARRY EMERSON FOSDICK

People in India are said to catch monkeys by setting out a small box with a tasty nut in it. On one side of the box is an opening

that is large enough for the monkey to reach in with his outstretched
hand but too small for him to withdraw the hand once he's clutched
the nut. When the monkey grabs the prize, he's caught. But he has a
choice: He can hold on to the nut and stay trapped, or he can let it
go and walk away from the box. Unenlightened little creatures that
they are, most monkeys hold on to the nut, making it easy for hunt-
ers to pick them up—box, nut, and all.

Hard as it is to admit, you and I have been known to get
caught in the same kind of trap. Sometimes when we feel
controlled, we need to look around us to see if we have been like
the monkey. Maybe we are holding on to something,
but in doing so, we stay trapped.

Jerry has been married for more than a decade
to an energetic woman who is vigilant about controlling their social calendar. Not only does she schedule
dinner parties in their home most months, but she
also volunteers for countless civic events and activities. She coordinates the school auction. She's in charge of their
church's bake sale, and on and on. This all was fine with her easygoing husband until her frenetic pace kept him from having time
for himself. In a counseling session, he confided: "She tells me
where and when I'm supposed to be someplace most evenings
and on most weekends. And if I don't follow through, she lays on
the guilt. It's driving me nuts."

Control is a hard-edged
word; it has—at least it
seems to have—no
poetry in it.

Judith Viorst

Jerry went on to tell me that he had given up golf and other
enjoyable activities because of her controlling ways. He sat in my
office, weary and depressed. As he contemplated his life, he felt that
the only way he could gain freedom from his wife's control was to
let go of his marriage.

Well, it didn't take long for us to come up with other choices
Jerry could make—choices that gave him back his freedom and
allowed him to enjoy the marriage he truly cherished. Through
our discussions, he realized that what he was really holding on to
was his peace-at-all-costs attitude. He had been afraid to speak up

to his wife, to reclaim some control over his own life. When Jerry chose to practice some of the strategies outlined in the rest of this book, he regained some of his freedom, and today he is one of the most happily married men I know. And his happiness is the result of his choice to let go of something that was trapping him—not his marriage, as he had first believed, but his unwillingness to speak up to his wife.

> One's philosophy is not best expressed in words; it is expressed in the choices one makes. . . . The process never ends until we die. And the choices we make are ultimately our responsibility.
>
> ELEANOR ROOSEVELT

I heard a similar story when I recently ran into a woman I hadn't seen for a while. "Georgia, how are you?" I asked.

She began to pour out her story of working in an office of Control Freaks. "It was unbearable. I felt so trapped, and I could see only one way out: quitting. But before I did that, I talked over my situation with a friend, hoping my friend could see some choices that weren't so apparent to me. My friend encouraged me to confront my boss, to tell her what it felt like to work under her controlling style. When I thought about it, I realized that I really had nothing to lose. I had already decided that I was prepared to quit if things didn't improve. If I ended up leaving because my boss would refuse to hear me out, then at least I had exercised all my choices."

Georgia did confront her boss. It was not pleasant. Her boss was quite resistant at first, but as a result of Georgia's persistence the boss agreed to some changes that would give Georgia more respect and freedom. In the end, she was able to stay at her job.

> The difficulty in life is the choice.
>
> GEORGE MOORE

Jerry and Georgia, unlike the monkeys in India, made positive choices that gave them freedom. You, too, can make a choice. Yes, you can *choose* to be treated differently. We'll get to that in practical terms in part 2 of this book.

The point is that no one can control you—only God is in true control. People may coerce, seduce, cajole, threaten, and tempt you. But they cannot control you in the sense of actually making you do something against your will (by the way, even God won't do that—as Leon Morris said, "God has no need for marionettes"). It comes down to choices. You may feel that you are being controlled, but look carefully. Is that true? Do you have no option but to be pressed into acting contrary to your own desires? Are you like a monkey, feverishly holding on to your "prize" because you won't give up what you see as your only option for getting something you want?

> When you have to make a choice and don't make it, that is in itself a choice.
>
> WILLIAM JAMES

Let me assure you that there are many options for coping with controlling people. And the bulk of this book is devoted to spelling them out. In fact, in many cases, the strategy may help you escape the annoyance of control without having to give up whatever it is you are holding on to.

FEELING UNEASY?

One more thought before leaving this chapter. Maybe you're feeling nervous. Perhaps you're thinking that *you* are the Control Freak. Or worse, maybe someone close to you has told you so. Perhaps that's the reason you're reading this book. Well, rest easy. As I've said before, nearly everyone is a Control Freak some of the time. But at the risk of sounding controlling, let's put that on hold. We'll diagnose you and get to what you can do to keep your controlling tendencies under control in part 3 of this book. After reading the remainder of part 1, you may even want to skip part 2 and go directly to part 3 if you like. Regardless, it is important that we next consider what the Control Freak looks like—in you or in someone else.

> God gave us a free choice because there is no significance to love that knows no alternative.
>
> JAMES C. DOBSON

3

THE ANATOMY OF A CONTROL FREAK

It seems easier to be God than to love God, easier to control people than to love people.

HENRI NOUWEN

Stephen Fagan always needed to be in charge. When he bought a house that needed extensive renovations, he oversaw the work himself. He ordered his second wife, Barbara, to say "I love you" into the phone whenever he called. He demanded that she stand in the front window each day and wave until he drove out of sight. It was all part of his carefully constructed world—a world of compulsive control that began falling apart in the spring of 1998. That's when Fagan was arrested at his Palm Beach mansion for the 1979 kidnapping of his own baby daughters from a previous marriage after a bitter divorce. While Fagan says he rescued his girls from a neglectful mother, his first and second wives claim Stephen was a Control Freak who went way, way too far.

And it's hard to argue with their assessment. Who wouldn't agree that Stephen Fagan was a categorical Control Freak (not to mention a full-blown psychopath)? You don't need to be a clinical psychologist to see that this guy's controlling tendencies were way out of control. All the signs were there. Most Control Freaks, however, the ones you and I rub shoulders with, are not nearly that obvious. Still, if you know what to look for, Control Freaks become relatively easy to spot.

THE TOP TEN QUALITIES OF A CONTROL FREAK

In this chapter we take a close look at the most common characteristics of Control Freaks—whether these characteristics are clearly evident or lurking more subtly beneath the surface. Of course, the most obvious and overarching characteristic of these people is the desperate desire to be in control. But there's more to this desire than meets the eye. Most Control Freaks are obnoxious, tenacious, invasive, obsessive, perfectionistic, critical, irritable, demanding, rigid, and closeminded.

Obnoxious

Control Freaks are often obnoxious. The word *obnoxious* comes from the Latin *noxius,* which means hurtful. And many Control Freaks cause harm. They injure nearly every relationship they have because of their controlling and destructive ways.

Tim, a new professor fresh out of graduate school, is a good example. I observed him for almost four years at the university where I teach. Wanting to make a good impression on his dean and his colleagues, Tim made every effort to follow his job description to the letter. He always arrived at his classes well ahead of schedule, worked hard to mentor students outside of class, attended every faculty meeting and kept fastidious notes on the proceedings, published respectable articles in leading journals, volunteered his services in the community, and submitted quarterly reports of his accomplishments to his dean. He was a model scholar and superb professor.

But Tim had a problem. He expected everyone around him, even senior-ranking faculty members, to do the same things he did. Tim never hid his opinions. He felt obliged to point out his colleagues' foibles and make suggestions on how they could improve. He once told me in no uncertain terms that I was disrespecting my students if I didn't wear a tie to class. He would sometimes quote, verbatim, rules and regulations from the faculty handbook to show how others weren't pulling their weight. He was a stickler for proper procedure in meetings, often hurting others' feelings with his desire to follow *Robert's Rules of Order*. And, if that weren't enough, Tim would often point to casual statements made by his fellow professors in a previous meeting, statements he had recorded in his notebook, and show them how they were inconsistent or misleading. In short, Tim was a Control Freak, and his most outstanding quality was being obnoxious. Nobody, but nobody, seemed to enjoy his company.

> Selfish persons are incapable of loving others, but they are not capable of loving themselves either.
>
> ERICH FROMM

In case you are wondering, Tim (not his real name) never made it to tenured status. His colleagues dismissed his application out of hand, in spite of his long list of professional accomplishments, because of a "lack of collegiality." The dismissal report could have just as easily, but not nearly as politely, said he was an obnoxious Control Freak who didn't get along with others. And nobody would have disagreed.

Tenacious

A little boy was on the back porch playing somewhat roughly with his reluctant cat. When they got to making a sizable commotion, the boy's mother heard it and hollered to him, "Johnny, are you pulling the cat's tail?"

"No, Mama," the little boy said, "I'm just holding her tail. She's doing all the pulling."

Control Freaks are a lot like Johnny. If someone suggests a new way of doing something, for example, they fiercely resist by holding on to the way they want things done, no matter how loud the commotion.

"Stubborn" is another way to describe them. I know a Control Freak who will stick to his opinion like a pit bull holding on to a bone. It doesn't matter how illogical his argument or how insignificant his point, he won't let go. It's part of the Control Freak code: "Don't ever, ever, ever give in." This fellow, for example, could easily spend several minutes correcting a story you are telling because he's convinced that when you said it happened on a Monday, it was really a Wednesday. No matter that it makes absolutely no difference to the story—he wants to be right. Even when you loudly protest, he won't let go of his point until you give in or give up.

> Those who control their anger have great understanding; those with a hasty temper will make mistakes.
>
> PROVERBS 14:29

Once Control Freaks set their sights on a particular point or goal, there is no arguing them out of it. Compromise is unspeakable. They are right, and everyone else is wrong. Period. End of discussion.

Nineteenth-century clergyman Henry Ward Beecher must have had Control Freaks in mind when he said, "The difference between perseverance and obstinacy is that one comes from a strong will, and the other from a strong won't."

Invasive

I once counseled a man who grew up with a controlling father who wanted to know everything about his son's life—where the boy went, whom he was with, what he read, how he spent his money. But the father's control went beyond even this. He regularly went through his son's room, taking careful inventory of his son's belongings, rifling through the boy's knapsack and desk drawers.

Like this father, most Control Freaks have little respect for privacy and often snoop in areas that aren't their business. Some Control Freaks exhibit their invasive quality not so much by snooping in other's belongings but by poking around in people's private lives. "How much did you pay for that watch?" they will ask boldly. "Is it true that your brother might be losing his job?" Or, "Tell me what's happening with you and your husband. I notice you don't sit together in church anymore." Probing. Searching. Inspecting. Hunting. Some Control Freaks will do whatever it takes to get personal or private information that's none of their business.

Speaking of church, I've seen some "saintly" Control Freaks who cloak their invasiveness in religious talk. "Why has the Lord put you on my heart?" they may ask as a way of getting their gossip fix. Or, "I want to pray for you, but I need to know what's really going on in your life." Not that every concerned parishioner is trying to invade your privacy, but Control Freaks often are out of control in their need to know.

Invasive strategies and techniques come in all stripes and colors. But whatever form they take, you can be assured that experienced Control Freaks have used most of them. Why? Because information is power. And the more power Control Freaks have, the better they feel. So they dig and pry into other people's lives, invading places where we have all but placed signs that read Private or Keep Out. But Control Freaks don't think these signs apply to them.

Obsessive

A friend recently told me of an experience he had at a luncheon with several dozen business leaders. They had come together to hear from a reputable economist who would be giving a speech about the recession. On a large flip chart, the speaker made a black spot in the middle of the paper and asked a man in the front row what he saw. The man replied promptly, "A black spot." The speaker asked every person the same question. One by one, each replied, "A black spot."

> A point of view can be a dangerous luxury when substituted for insight and understanding.
>
> MARSHALL MCLUHAN

With calm and deliberate emphasis the speaker then walked pensively across the small platform, paused, then said: "Yes, there is a little black spot. But none of you mentioned the large sheet of white paper it is on." The speaker then stepped to the podium, gathered his notes, said "Thank you," and sat down.

My friend who attended the luncheon said the room was shockingly quiet for a few moments as the speaker took his seat, and the host, who was seated on the platform, looked nervously around, not knowing what to do next. Then one person in the back began to applaud. Then another. Soon every businessperson in the room was clapping for the speaker. What had he taught them about the recession? That you've got to have perspective. You can't focus on one small thing or one brief moment. You've got to see the big picture and put things in context.

The message from this daring speaker was simple but profound. It's a valuable lesson for everyone, but it's wasted on nearly every Control Freak. You see, most Control Freaks are not interested in the big picture. They most often zero in on some minor detail that prevents them from seeing anything else. They may have a suspicion that something is going wrong in a relationship, for example, so they become obsessed over every nuance of conversation and unintended gesture that the other person makes. They can't seem to focus on anything other than the possible relationship rift.

At work Control Freaks may focus exclusively on one particular problem that causes them to lose sight of other issues that are more important. They may become so consumed by the amount of space old files are taking up, for example, that they do not get to the job at hand because they are too busy trying to convince everyone that something needs to be done to purge the files. Or they may fear their upcoming job-performance review will give them less than perfect marks, so they become obsessed about the possibilities and repercussions of a poor review—which may not even occur.

He who wants to blame, finds the sugar sour.

GERMAN PROVERB

Control Freaks become obsessed about anything and everything: a person's offhand remark, a mistake at the pharmacy, where people are seated around a conference table, their child's friends, a remark they said last week to an associate on the phone, and on and on. Anything can become their "black spot" as they lose perspective and neglect the big picture.

Aldous Huxley, the British author, summed up this obsessive quality this way: "Single-mindedness is all very well in cows or baboons; in an animal claiming to belong to the same species as Shakespeare, it is simply disgraceful."

Perfectionistic

Listen carefully, and you will hear Control Freaks say under their breath, "I can't believe I did that. What a jerk." They will berate themselves for not having everything go exactly the way they wanted it to. "I can't believe I forgot my cell phone." "Why didn't I plan for rain?" "I should have known the bank would close early today."

We all get frustrated from time to time because something throws a monkey wrench into the works, but typical Control Freaks can't let it go. Since the bank is closed when they thought it would be open, they punish themselves (or get mad at the bank) and focus on how they have now thrown off their entire day. "I really needed to deposit this money today," they might say. You ask the logical question: "Did you write a check that might bounce since you didn't get to make the deposit?" And they respond: "No, no. I just really wanted to get this off my to-do list, and I was sure the bank was open. Why can't I remember it closes at six on Thursdays?"

Control Freaks demand perfection of themselves and everyone else. Few things are "good enough." If you live with Control Freaks, you know this too well. Their perfectionistic ways set standards you never agreed to live by. It may not matter to you that the pillows on the couch need to be angled in the corner just so, but it does to them, and you better figure that out. Right? Or maybe you could care less when the gas gauge in your family car goes below its halfway point, but you've learned that your Control Freak spouse doesn't like it. So you oblige and fill it up when you notice the red needle heading toward empty. You do this and countless other things to appease the perfectionistic Control Freak.

> We might remind ourselves that criticism is as inevitable as breathing.
>
> T. S. ELIOT

I love what the French writer François Fénelon had to say about perfection. "It is only imperfection that complains of what is imperfect. The more perfect we are, the more gentle and quiet we become toward the defects of others." As a recovering Control Freak myself, I confess that I take these words to heart.

Critical

I've often been puzzled by people who make their living from being critical. How do they get away with some of the things they say? Movie critics, for example, can lambaste a film that ends up being a box-office smash, and the critic's reputation isn't even tarnished. On a recent cross-country flight to Washington, D.C., I read a book review that completely panned the author's efforts. The critic's comments made me curious. So during my layover in Chicago, I dashed into the airport bookstore and read the first couple of pages. I got hooked. I bought the book and thoroughly enjoyed it on the rest of my flight.

As I said, I've often been puzzled by professional critics. In fact, I've made a habit of collecting "bad" reviews. One of my favorites is of the original 1946 Broadway production of *Annie Get Your Gun*. One critic wrote, "Irving Berlin's score is musically not exciting or even tuneful." *Annie Get Your Gun* ended up being Berlin's greatest stage success, running more than a thousand performances on Broadway and popularizing such hits as "There's No Business Like Show Business" and "Anything You Can Do." When *Fiddler on the Roof* came out, a respected critic said, "It seems clear this is no smash hit." It became the third-longest run in Broadway history. When the movie *Gone with the Wind* came into theaters, one critic summed it up by saying, "No Civil War picture ever made a nickel." And in 1964, when Ronald Reagan was up for a starring role in a movie to play the president of the United States, a critic said, "Reagan doesn't have the presidential look."

Surely these critics must have lost their jobs, right? Hardly. It seems being critical, even when your criticism is unwarranted or off base, doesn't always do that much damage. It's just part of the job. But when unsolicited criticism comes from an unpaid Control

Freak, you can be assured that damage will be done. Anyone who
has to live or work with a critic who isn't collecting a paycheck for
being critical knows what I mean. Control Freaks can
be some of the most painfully critical people you'll
ever meet. It seems they can't keep their critical
comments in check. They blurt out their judgments as
easily as a professional reviewer gives a thumbs-down
to a movie.

> Be aware that rigidity
> imprisons.
>
> MADELEINE L'ENGLE

The question is *why*. Why do Control Freaks impose their
critical comments so freely? As one who can be prone to critical
comments myself, I'll tell you why. Control Freaks often think
their criticisms will somehow make something or someone better.
Of course, they never do, but this doesn't keep them from trying
to control through criticism. "Those black shoes don't do much
for your outfit," a Control Freak might say. "You would look
better wearing brown flats with that skirt." Of course, the friend
puts on the brown shoes. Or in the case of a marriage: "I'm
embarrassed to pull up in front of our house with so many weeds
in our lawn," a controlling wife might say to her husband. Guess
who gets right to work in the yard?

If you're puzzled by this Control Freak trait, wonder no
more. You see, criticism is a terrific tool for getting people to do
what the Control Freaks want them to do.

Irritable

Cranky and contentious. Touchy and testy. These are the kinds of
words that pop into people's minds to describe Roberta. She
works with a large real estate agency just outside of Houston. She
is successful. Very successful. For three years straight, Roberta
was the top sales agent in the city. How did she do it? By working longer and harder than almost everyone else. Roberta is also
a self-confessed Control Freak who oversees *every* aspect of the
sales she makes, for both the buyer and the seller. She doesn't
want anyone else in her office making a mistake that would

reflect badly on her, so she handles everything herself. But at a price: She is also known as the most irascible and irritable person within miles.

People who work with Roberta know to walk around on eggshells if they don't want to set her off. The tiniest of things can ruin her day—and everyone else's too. One time she sulked all afternoon because the district manager of her agency came through town and did not invite her to a lunch meeting. On another occasion, she became cranky because the battery on her cell phone would not recharge properly. She once chewed out a colleague because a Sold sign wasn't posted on a property the day she requested it to be. When a train caused her to be late for a meeting with a potential buyer at a property, she actually honked at the passing train—as if it would go faster—and then whined about it all afternoon back in the office. The examples could go on, but the point is that Roberta, like so many other Control Freaks, is a very irritable person.

> The camel never sees its own hump, but its neighbor's hump is ever before its eyes.
>
> ARABIAN PROVERB

When Control Freaks don't get their way, they let you know. They seem to have no ability to go with the flow. When they encounter opposition, they become cross, crabby, and cranky. Little things tick them off: a messy top on a bottle of ketchup, a car that is parked on the "wrong" side of the driveway, a flashlight not being where it is "supposed" to be, and on and on. For Control Freaks, anything and everything can be cause for a tantrum.

Demanding

"Jenny, give me that!" Dan yelled at his wife. When she refused to hand over her paycheck at his command, he yelled again. Frustrated that she didn't immediately respond to his bark, he tried to grab the check from her hand. Jenny had a good hold on it, and before they knew it, the check ripped. Jenny was tired of jumping at Dan's every order, and Dan responded in characteristic Control Freak style: by demanding.

Many Control Freaks are like Dan. To get their way, they often resort to insisting and coercing other people to do things. Like a kidnapper who is trying to secure a ransom, Control Freaks order people around. In addition to trying to control the checkbook, Dan, for example, often snaps at Jenny to make his oatmeal in the morning. He insists that she never, ever touch the stereo equipment in their family room. Dan makes Jenny answer the phone in another room, so that she won't disturb him if he is watching a game on TV. He may even require Jenny to wear a certain outfit when they go to dinner with friends. No doubt about it, Dan is in charge.

Like a brigadier general controlling his troops, a Control Freak often shouts orders and expects everyone to follow them. If you live or work with this kind of person, you know how belittling, how demeaning it sometimes feels. And like Jenny, you may have tried to draw the line and put an end to being bossed around, but that doesn't stop most Control Freaks. They go right on commanding and demanding. They muster up a demanding demeanor, hoping it will keep them more in control. What the Control Freak doesn't understand is what Michel de Montaigne, the sixteenth-century French writer, said so eloquently: "He who establishes his argument by noise and command shows that his reason is weak."

Rigid

In the hugely successful television hit *Seinfeld*, one of the most popular episodes was based on a real-life situation. "The Soup Nazi" centered on a feisty man who ran a small eatery where New Yorkers stood outside in long lines to enjoy take-out orders of this cook's delicious soup creations. The catch? Customers had to put up with this Control Freak's rigid rules. Only one customer in the store at a time. Place your order immediately. Do not point. Don't ask questions. Pay and leave. If you wanted to feast on these tasty soups, you did as the man said. And if you didn't? "No soup for you," the Soup Nazi would snap. "Come back three months."

The episode struck a chord with viewers because we all know Control Freaks who live by rigid rules and expect us to do the same. And we may even know the feeling of wanting what a Control Freak has to offer and putting up with ridiculous demands in order to get it. My wife and I once hired a gardener who spoke mostly Russian. He did outstanding work. You couldn't find a weed in our yard if he had been there. He could get interesting things to grow in our planters. He trained the ivy to curl up our retaining wall the way we wanted. And the trees in our yard seemed to do whatever he commanded. The problem? He would never let us know when he would show up to do his work. Maybe next week or next month. Maybe never at all. We never knew. What's worse, he might leave midway through a project and not tell us when he would return. He was in charge of his schedule, and he worked only when he wanted to work. If we tried to get him to nail down a date, he would quickly snap, "No work dat way." He was rigid about it.

> The faultfinder is a person who has one sharp eye for faults and one blind eye for virtues.
>
> ANONYMOUS

Most Control Freaks are. They have one way of doing things— their way. Control Freaks can be as inflexible as drill sergeants in trying to force their methods on you. They want life to run a certain way and aren't willing to budge from their regimen. Their exacting details for preparing a salad (or soup), for driving a car, for raking leaves, and for doing anything else are not to be questioned. They "know" what's best for everyone and "allow" others to take the reins only if they follow the Control Freak's rules.

Closeminded

One more quality makes the top-ten list for Control Freaks. Most of these people are not interested in discussion. It's as if they have all the truth, and anyone who disagrees with them just doesn't know anything. They fail to recognize that only God has all the truth. They feel no need to examine both sides of any issue. Their mind is made up before they even hear that there *is* another side to an issue. So, they circle the wagons to protect their opinions and deny even an effort at clarification, balance, and understanding, to say nothing of building community with people who do not see things exactly as they do.

"My mind is made up, and there is no changing it," Ron said to all of us sitting around a conference table. We were in a board meeting discussing an agenda item that had potential to modify the direction in which this nonprofit organization we were representing was headed. Many of us felt the proposed change would benefit the organization. It would have allowed financial pressures to be lessened while still maintaining the core cause and mission of the organization. But Ron, the board chair, would hear nothing of it. He put an end to the conversation before it even got going.

> A cynic can chill and dishearten with a single word.
>
> RALPH WALDO EMERSON

"Won't you consider hearing from some of the committee members who have been studying this for more than a month?" a brave board member pressed him.

"I've read their report," said Ron. "I've heard their concerns, and I reject them. I've already told you why. Next item."

Ron's zeal for sticking to the organization's original mission was blinding him to how the original mission would be fulfilled and expanded if he would be open to hearing opinions that did not match his own. But like many Control Freaks, Ron refused. And he left many of us wondering why we, along with our opinions, were even needed.

A few days after I left that meeting, a fellow board member sent me a sad but thoughtful note in which he quoted English poet William Blake: "The man who never alters his opinion is like standing water and breeds reptiles of the mind." This fellow went on to say in his note that he was resigning because Ron's thinking

was too constricted, his mind too closed for hope of any potential
dialogue down the road.

Sadly, many Control Freaks close their mind before they
allow good thoughts to enter it. And ultimately, this causes them
to close their heart to people who would also like to have a place
in their life—if only there were room.

RATING THE TOP TEN QUALITIES OF CONTROL

I suppose the list of irritating qualities could go on and on. But in
my experience and in my many interviews with people who are
dealing with Control Freaks, these are the qualities that top the list.
You may find it helpful to personalize these qualities to your situation. Use the following scales to determine how much of each
quality the Control Freak in your life reveals. By the way, if you
identified more than one Control Freak in the test from chapter 2,
rate each person with the following scale:

Not Obnoxious   **Very Obnoxious**

         1   2   3   4   5

Not Tenacious   **Very Tenacious**

         1   2   3   4   5

Not Invasive   **Very Invasive**

         1   2   3   4   5

Not Obsessive   **Very Obsessive**

         1   2   3   4   5

Not Perfectionistic   **Very Perfectionistic**

         1   2   3   4   5

Not Critical   **Very Critical**

1   2   3   4   5

Not Irritable   **Very Irritable**

1   2   3   4   5

Not Demanding   **Very Demanding**

1   2   3   4   5

Not Rigid   **Very Rigid**

1   2   3   4   5

Not Closeminded   **Very Closeminded**

1   2   3   4   5

There is no scoring to this scale. It is simply designed to give you more awareness. By pinpointing the most disturbing qualities about the Control Freaks in your life, you will be better equipped to cope. You will know more precisely what about these people pushes your buttons. And this heightened awareness is the first step to designing your personal strategy for taming the Control Freaks in your life. You may also find it helpful to average the numbers from each of these scales to determine more clearly where these people are on a continuum of Control Freaks. In other words, add up the numbers you circled, and divide by 10. If the resulting number is a 1 or 2, the Control Freaks in your life are relatively mild. A 3 indicates a moderate degree of Control Freak tendencies, and a 4 or 5 means you know Control Freaks who are close to being off the charts.

> Rigidity clips the future's wings—then later criticizes it for not flying.
>
> CHARLES R. SWINDOLL

Before we move on to specific strategies for coping with

Control Freaks, I think it's important for us to step back for a minute and look at another significant issue regarding control: Is all control bad? It's very easy for us to react to the Control Freaks around us and conclude that all control is wrong. But is that true? What would our world be like without control or without self-control?

When we think of control in the context of annoying, controlling behavior, we can readily lose perspective and throw out the proverbial baby with the bathwater. While we don't want to do that, we do want to understand the difference between healthy control and overcontrol. These are some of the issues we'll explore in the next chapter.

4

IS ALL CONTROL BAD?

All those qualities that we call human derive from the possibility within every human being of acquiring control over the instinctual self.

SELMA FRAIBERG

Another day on the burn unit at the University of Washington School of Medicine. I was just a year or two out of graduate school, working as a medical psychologist in one of the most excruciating places imaginable. At any given moment throughout the day, I could hear patients of all ages moaning in agony or screaming in terror. The issue was pain. And lots of it. Because human nerve endings are located in the skin, burns are the most painful injuries sustainable. And the scrubbing of the skin to avoid infection seems like nothing short of human torture.

On this particular day, I was making rounds with my supervisor when he told me of an experiment that was revolutionizing pain management on the unit. For years the basic treatment was to administer pain medication whenever a patient screamed loudly enough—until the patient reached the maximum dosage. Once that level was reached, little else could be done. Patients lay helplessly suffering.

However, an experiment was changing the pain protocol in this hospital. Doctors gave a group of patients on the unit a simple apparatus that allowed them to administer their own pain medication whenever they desired. Rather than buzzing a nurse to give them more medicine, these patients squeezed a lever to relieve their own suffering. For the first time ever, the patients were in control of their own medication.

Did it make any difference? You bet. Not only was the screaming on the unit lowered by several decibels, but the researchers were also astonished to discover that the patients ended up using less medication than before. It seems that when patients are in control of their own dosage, they do not need as much medicine.

Control is a positive force in the management of physical pain. And it's a positive force in many areas of life. With this in mind, I dedicate this chapter to helping you see the good side of control. I've worked with many people who are trying to cope with Control Freaks, and I've seen too many of them write off the Control Freak completely. The problem with this is that these people truncate a relationship that has potential to become a positive force in their life.

HAPPY ARE THOSE IN CONTROL

Feeling in control is vital to mental and physical health. Psychologist Judith Rodin has demonstrated in experiments at Yale University how merely feeling in control can increase the functioning of a person's immune system.[1] Control is also critical to our happiness at home and our satisfaction at work. In fact, after reviewing a huge number of studies on what makes people happy, David Myers, author of *The Pursuit of Happiness*, discovered that feeling in control is one of the key traits of happy people. Of course, he is not saying that you can control everything about your life. The point is that the most happy people on the planet do not leave their lives up to chance or luck. They draw on God's enabling power to steer their boat with intention rather than being bandied about by random winds.

> Most powerful is he who has himself in his own power.
>
> SENECA

Control as a primary source of happiness, apparently, starts early in life. In an experiment with three groups of eight-week-olds, each infant was provided with a special air pillow that

responded to the pressure of its head by closing a switch. In one
group, let's call it group A, a mobile of colored balls hanging over
each infant's crib spun for one second whenever the
pillow was pressed. In group B the mobile also spun,
but its spinning did not depend on the infants'
actions. Group C was given a stabile, not a mobile,
and experienced neither movement nor control.

> I don't mind a control
> freak as long as he's
> using it to better himself
> and me. I stay away from
> these guys one-on-one.
> They're murder. Let them
> do the control thing on
> the organization.
>
> TERRY BRADSHAW

The infants of group A, having learned that they
could control the movements of the mobile, demonstrated their knowledge by greatly increasing the
number of times they pressed the pillow. The infants
in the other groups did not. Group A was also the only group in
which every infant—three or four days into the experiment—was
smiling and cooing.[2]

For young and old alike, controlling our surroundings
clearly brings pleasure. Just ask people who are not allowed to
adjust their room temperature, change their room lights, or move
the furniture in their living quarters. Chances are, they feel as if
they're in prison, or perhaps they actually are.

WHAT HAPPENS WHEN WE LOSE CONTROL?

Not only is control an important part of our ability to live well,
but *losing* control has a negative effect on our ability to function.
The loss of control is driving people into doctors'
offices with psychological and medical diseases, at
great human and economic cost. For example, college
students who believe they have little or no control
over what happens to them are far more likely to
become severely depressed or anxious than those

> Nothing is impossible for
> the man who doesn't
> have to do it himself.
>
> ANONYMOUS

students who believe they have a say in their circumstances.[3] The
same is true with the elderly. Two nurse researchers from Pennsylvania State University tested sixty men and women (age sixty-five
to ninety-five) who were residents in two long-term care facilities
in rural Pennsylvania. The residents who believed that what

happened to them was controlled more by chance than by their own actions had much lower self-esteem.[4] A study at Massachusetts General Hospital in Boston showed that surgery patients who are taught how to control their abdominal muscles to avoid spasm after surgery are discharged from the hospital an average of three days sooner than patients who don't learn this method of control.[5]

Whether it be in a hospital, a nursing home, or a college classroom, helpless people often perceive control to be beyond them, and this perception deepens their resignation. This is precisely what researcher Martin Seligman and others found in experiments with both animals and people.[6] When dogs were strapped in a harness and given repeated shocks with no opportunity to avoid them, they felt helpless—obviously. But later, when the dogs were placed in a situation in which they *could* escape the punishment by merely leaping a hurdle, these same dogs cowered without hope. Faced with traumatic events over which they have no control, people also come to feel helpless and hopeless. This was discovered near the end of World War II, when death camp prisoners were being released only to discover they could have easily escaped on their own through holes in fences and unlocked gates. It's what researchers call "learned helplessness." And it's the price we pay for giving up control—a price, by the way, too many people who live and work with chronic Control Freaks have paid.

> Everything can be taken from a man but one thing: the last of human freedoms—to choose one's attitude in any given set of circumstances, to choose one's own way.
>
> VIKTOR FRANKL

THE CHOICE IS YOURS

Whether or not you are in control does not seem to be the ultimate issue. It's whether you *believe* you have control that really counts. Think about it. Since we can reduce the intensity of our stress by simply thinking about our problems in a more positive light (without seeing them as catastrophes), we have within us the ability to control the effect that adversity has on us. Jill Kinmont,

who was once the country's top female skier, is a great example.
She became a quadriplegic when she fell and severed her spine in
a race just before her twentieth birthday. When she
was forty-one, she was asked what accounted for her
bright and positive outlook on life. Was it, the ques-
tioner suggested, because she had nineteen great years
in the beginning? "I beg your pardon," she replied.
"I've had forty-one great years."

> The proverb warns that
> "You should not bite the
> hand that feeds you."
> But maybe you should, if
> it prevents you from
> feeding yourself.
>
> THOMAS SZASZ

Can you imagine the price Jill would have paid
if she had given up her ability to choose her own attitude? Can you imagine the price any of us pays when we surrender our life without making deliberate choices? John Milton was
right when he said we "can make a heav'n of hell, a hell of
heav'n." The choice is ours.

I want to be sure I make this point clear. All of us have the
wide-open option of choosing the ways we will cope with life. We
are influenced by culture, no doubt. Our family and other significant people in our lives, including Control Freaks, certainly shape
us. But the attitudes we finally choose to live by are internalized as
our own. And with the help of God we can choose to take control
and make those attitudes whatever we desire.

THE BIOLOGY OF CONTROL

Okay. We've established that control can be a good thing. The
helplessness we suffer as a result of giving it up is not worth the
price of the pain. But what does it take to cultivate healthy control
without becoming a Control Freak? The answer
comes in understanding what goes on inside of us
when we lose control and in learning how to handle
our impulses.

> Humanity cannot be cut
> adrift from its own
> biology, but neither is it
> enchained by it.
>
> ROSE LEWONTIN

Remember when Mike Tyson bit off a chunk of
Evander Holyfield's ear during their 1997 heavy-
weight boxing title match? Why did Tyson do it? Because he
became enraged and lost control, right? Well, those who study the

architecture of the human brain put it a little differently. Tyson, they say, was hijacked by his brain's *amygdala*—the alarm circuitry that makes us "snap" in emotional emergencies.

The amygdala is the brain's emotional memory bank. It uses stored memories to scan incoming information and determines whether there is a potential threat. In Tyson's case, the head butting by Holyfield flooded Tyson with angry memories of an earlier match that he also lost. The upshot for Tyson was an instantaneous reaction that eventually cost him $3 million. All because he gave in to a primal impulse.

It's downright chilling to see the effects of losing control. In New York a man shot and killed an employee of a video store after the victim refused to refund the quarter the shooter had lost in a pay telephone. A Boston insurance executive was charged with murdering his wife after she chided him for having overcooked some pasta. These may be extreme examples of what can happen when the human brain is hijacked by the amygdala, but they serve as reminders for how deadly life is without control. Every day we read bizarre headlines that cry out for us to stay in control. The question is, how do we do that?

> When we can't walk one more step and yet we keep walking, when we learn something new by practicing every day, when we give ourselves over to blistering rage or to passion, when we fall off our diet and into the crème brûlée, . . . when we force our nearest and dearest to do it our way, we are—though perhaps we don't know it, or perhaps we call it another name—taking, or giving up, or abusing control.
>
> JUDITH VIORST

THE PATH TO HEALTHY CONTROL

In his best-selling book *Emotional Intelligence*, Daniel Goleman discusses "a microcosm of the eternal battle between impulse and restraint, id and ego, desire and self-control, gratification and delay." He's talking about the famous "marshmallow test," in which four-year-olds are offered this deal: They may, if they wish, eat a marshmallow immediately. Or, if they can wait until the tester returns, they will then be permitted to eat two marshmallows. Some four-year-olds, not surprisingly, grab the single marshmallow almost as soon as the tester leaves the room, while others—valiantly fighting off temptation—hold out for fifteen or twenty minutes until the tester returns, winning their well-earned two-marshmallow prize.

When the two-marshmallow children were eval- uated during their adolescence, they were measured against their one-marshmallow peers and found to be more confident, more competent, more assertive, more reliable, and less likely—when faced with difficulties—to quit, not to mention more eager to learn, better able to concentrate, and better able to achieve higher scores on the SATs. In addition, they continued to be far better at self-control.[7]

> Self-control excels control of the beast.
>
> AFRICAN PROVERB

The lesson is simple: We cannot be in control of ourselves and our lives unless we learn to defer gratification. Whether we are the Control Freak or simply living around one, we find the path to healthy control by putting a clamp on our primal impulses and keeping our cool.

Just how well you keep your cool depends in large part on how well you can identify your own feelings. The more accurately you can monitor your emotional upsets, for example, the sooner you can recover from distress. This was shown in an experiment that had people watch a very graphic film about drunk-driving accidents. During the half hour after the film, viewers reported feeling distressed and depressed, with their thoughts repeatedly going back to the troubling scenes they had witnessed. The people quickest to recover were those with the greatest clarity about their feelings. Emotional clarity, it seems, enables us to control our bad moods.

> No two men see the world exactly alike, and different temperaments will apply in different ways a principle that they both acknowledge. The same man will, indeed, often see and judge the same things differently on different occasions: early convictions must give way to more mature ones.
>
> JOHANN WOLFGANG VON GOETHE

WHEN HEALTHY CONTROL BECOMES OVERCONTROL

Most people would agree that a sense of control is necessary for good emotional and physical health. But when people use control to dominate everything around them—other people, their environment, all situations and circumstances—then they have crossed the boundary into overcontrol. The key is being smart enough to know when to use your control and when not to. This, perhaps, is the make-or-break characteristic of being a Control Freak.

Controlling too much creates as much stress as feeling that you have no control at all. Type-A personalities, for example, are notorious for their need for control and equally notorious for their high risk of heart disease.[8] In their pursuit of dominance, Control Freaks often subject themselves to rigid routines that prevent them from enjoying life, to say nothing of the frustration they cause the people around them.

The bulk of this book is dedicated to harnessing that control, whether it be in a Meddling Manager, a Coercive Colleague, a Supervising Spouse, a Pushy Parent, an Invasive In-Law, a Tenacious Teen—or in you.

Before we get to the specifics of doing just that, however, I have one other question to answer. Why do Control Freaks take a good thing too far? It's what I call the soul of control, and in the next chapter we will look into its depths.

5

WHY CONTROL FREAKS ACT THE WAY THEY DO

Without self-confidence we are as babes in the cradles. And how can we generate this imponderable quality, which is yet so invaluable most quickly? By thinking that other people are inferior to oneself.

VIRGINIA WOOLF

As I write these words, my ten-month-old son has been sitting just a few feet from me in a newfangled baby contraption called a Supersaucer that, for an infant, offers more entertaining attractions and activities than a day at Disneyland. But a few minutes ago, baby John let out a piercing shriek that definitely signaled distress. My weary wife came running, saw his outstretched arms, and picked him up to cuddle. "You're getting tired and sleepy, little boy, aren't you? Or are you hungry?" she asked him as she swayed him back and forth. His crying stopped immediately.

Having just watched this interaction, it occurs to me that from the moment we arrive in this world, one of our primary tasks is to gain control. Our first job in life is to gain power over our autonomic system and develop motor skills to influence our surroundings. This allows us to pay attention to the oohs and coos of the person who cuddles us. And through our emerging ability to respond to others, we can elicit other desirable behaviors. Little by little, we learn to actively control our surroundings.

"Sometimes I want to be jiggled or tickled or patted," says the teeny tiny baby in Amy Schwartz's children's book. And "sometimes I want to ride in my Snuglie or in my stroller . . . my swing or my sling." And "sometimes I just want to be left to my own devices."[1]

In ten months' time, our baby, John, has learned to make his wishes pretty well known. Day or night, we gladly jump to meet his needs. Holding and rocking, feeding and cleaning, we have adapted our life rhythms to accommodate him any way we can. We've changed schedules, rearranged furniture. We can't resist the charms of his coos, cries, and grins. We are eagerly alert to his slightest cues. And I think he knows it. At least we hope he does.

TWO PATHS LEADING TO OVERCONTROL

As a psychologist, I know full well that if the care and attention we give to baby John is sufficiently in sync with his needs, he will have a decent chance of developing a burgeoning sense of personal effectiveness, a sense that he can make things happen. A healthy sense of control.

> Nothing is more terrible than activity without insight.
>
> THOMAS CARLYLE

"Human infants," writes psychologist Martin Seligman, "begin life more helpless than infants of any other species. In the course of the next decade or two, some acquire a sense of mastery over their surroundings; others acquire a profound sense of helplessness."[2] Which category we wind up in, he argues, depends on how often and how intensely we experience either impotence or control.

Dr. Seligman also argues that the lack of a steadfast parenting presence in our lives is a powerful source of early, deep, and repeatedly confirmed feelings of helplessness. Without it, there is no one to reliably respond to our shrieks and smiles. There is no one to give us a sense that what we do matters or makes a difference in what happens. An infant with an absent or inattentive parent suffers not only from a lack of love but also from what Seligman calls "a particularly crucial lack of control."

Without a responsive parent-figure, we may come to believe that taking action is meaningless, that we can't affect events, that we are helpless. And with this flimsy foundation for adult life, we generally fall into two temptations: We either give up and give in to a life of passivity, or we end up overcompensating by becoming full-blown Control Freaks.

But here's the rub: Even having the most nurturing and empowering parents in the world does not prevent these same overcontrolling tendencies from emerging. There are no guarantees on parental behavior—and this very fact, by the way, generates more overcontrolling behavior in some parents. The point is, almost everyone is equally likely to cultivate controlling tendencies.

> Don't touch me! Don't question me! Don't speak to me! Stay with me!
>
> SAMUEL BECKETT

Why? Sooner or later every one of us is hit over the head by an illusion of our own making. It is the illusion of control, which shatters into a million pieces as we come of age. Even if we were fortunate enough to have parents who were steadfast and nurturing, the illusion exists. You see, we developed a belief that we are all-powerful, and we developed this belief without even knowing it. We grew up with an illusion that our parents' powers are ours to share and that these powers give us complete control of our ourselves and the world. Reality, however, confronts us with the end of the illusion. As we mature, we realize we're far less powerful and far more vulnerable than we had ever imagined. So we sometimes cling to the illusion, trying desperately to put back the pieces by once again cultivating overcontrolling tendencies.

It's a tendency that toddlers can get away with. But it looks bad on an adult.

THE SOUL OF EVERY CONTROL FREAK IS RIDDLED WITH ANXIETY

Lillian is in her late thirties and likes to run the show. When she goes out with friends, she chooses the day, the time, and the restaurant. If that isn't enough, once the restaurant host selects a table, Lillian almost always requests a different one. Her friends have come to call it the "Lillian switch." She even tells her companions what to eat, and she dominates the flow of conversation. If Lillian doesn't get her way, she picks apart the place that her friends select or spends the evening sulking.

A few of Lillian's friends put up with her controlling ways, but many people go as fast as they come. Surely she knows what her dictatorial behavior does to people, so why does she do it? The answer is found, as it is with most Control Freaks, at a level more unconscious than conscious. Deep down, Lillian fears being vulnerable. She is anxious. She fears losing control altogether.

> In a world we find terrifying, we ratify that which doesn't threaten us.
>
> DAVID MAMET

Deep in the soul of every Control Freak is an ample supply of anxiety, a seemingly endless stream that continually fuels the fear of being out of control. Control Freaks can't relax because they feel at risk of being criticized or shamed for making an error. To feel safe, they feel that they have to be superhuman twenty-four hours a day. They have to master every situation, from the bedroom to the boardroom. The strain of constantly trying to keep from failing pushes them more and more into trying to control everything and everybody.

> Men are afraid to rock the boat in which they hope to drift safely through life's currents, when, actually, the boat is stuck on a sandbar. They would be better off to rock the boat and try to shake it loose, or, better still, jump into the water and swim for the shore.
>
> THOMAS SZASZ

If you are a self-confessed Control Freak, you know just what I mean. Though few people around you suspect it, you're well aware of the worry and distress that too often plague your days. On the one hand, you must live up to the impossible self-image you have created for yourself (strong, competent, etc.), but on the other hand, you deeply doubt your ability to do it. Anxiety is the result. And you know how anxiety fuels your desire to create a world that runs just the way you want it to. You know how it causes you to compulsively control not only your environment but also the people in it. You count on their compliance. You get frustrated when their needs and feelings interfere with your own. The result is more anxiety, and that fuels more unhealthy attempts to control it. You long to relax. To let down your guard. To be who you really are without fear of failure or rejection.

And if you're reading this book primarily because you're trying to manage a Control Freak in your life, you may have no idea how powerful anxiety can be. You may not be aware that when people feel vulnerable and unsafe, they resort to drastic measures for alleviating that anxiety. They control whatever and whomever they can in an attempt to subdue their worries and keep their fears at bay. Imagine an anxious man desperately holding on to a life ring to keep from drowning. The anxiety that shoots through his body strengthens his grip as he holds fast to the life ring. In the same way, Control Freaks are grabbing for anything and anybody that will keep them afloat as their personal anxiety rises.

> Anxiety does not empty tomorrow of its sorrow but only empties today of its strength.
>
> CHARLES HADDON SPURGEON

Anxiety, of course, is not all bad. Without it there would be no growth, no progress. Soon after we are born, anxiety provides motivation to act. And in moderation, anxiety is completely benevolent, a gift from God to prevent us from being totally complacent vegetables. But when the level of anxiety is out of proportion to the situation, controlling tendencies emerge. And the longer they linger, the more likely they are to create a full-blown Control Freak.

> There is hardly anyone so insignificant that he does not seem imposing to someone at some time.
>
> CHARLES HORTON COOLEY

Because of their anxiety, Control Freaks simply don't know when and where to stop. Look at it this way: Imagine what life would be like if everything we wanted and every goal we hoped to achieve were left to chance, the winds of fate, or other people's whims. The prospect of such utter powerlessness would be terrifying. Well, imaginary or not, that's what life is like for the hypercontrolling person.

Control Freaks on the farthest end of the controlling continuum (as measured in chapter 2) are trying so hard to control everything (even the weather), they lose control of themselves without warning. It's the story of the Control Freak golfer who goes berserk after slicing a drive. He hurls his driver down the fairway, takes another club out of his bag, and snaps it in two over his knee. Some Control Freaks literally "freak out."

JELLYFISH IN ARMOR

Cliff was promoted to the top tier of a large manufacturing company, bringing with him a reputation as a take-charge turnaround artist because of the ruthless reengineering and job cutting he had conducted in the past when the company was on the brink of bankruptcy. Cliff was as confident as they come. His very presence demanded respect, and he knew it. His hair-trigger anger and impatience had become his trademark, if not his tools. He knew how to crack the whip. And everyone talked about it—behind his back. But not everyone knew that underneath Cliff's gruff, intimidating, and controlling demeanor was a weak and fragile spirit.

> Anxiety is the *élan vital* which we carry with us, and which becomes stagnated if we are unsure about the role we have to play.
>
> FREDERICK S. PERLS

Cliff discovered the truth himself shortly after an especially loud and public blowup he had with one of the company's best managers. The problem was no longer avoidable. Good people were looking to join competing companies just to avoid his controlling ways. That's when an executive coach was called in to consult with Cliff on the way he was treating employees.

> Self-respect—The secure feeling that no one, as yet, is suspicious.
>
> H. L. MENCKEN

As part of her standard procedure, the consultant videotaped Cliff in action over the course of two days and then replayed the tape for him in private. The consultant pointed out specific and subtle behaviors, like the effect his forbidding facial expression had on people. But Cliff just couldn't see it. The competitive striving that had taken him to the top had become so habitual that he couldn't admit his own weakness, his own vulnerability. He had built a fortress around his fragile feelings. He had a tough exterior but his emotional soul was riddled with anxiety and fear of failure.

Cliff is like a lot of Control Freaks. They are not nearly as self-assured as they often appear. Terrified of being criticized, rejected, or exposed in any way, they try to protect themselves by staying in control of every aspect of their lives—and everyone else's.

Let me say it simply. The soul of control is fueled by anxiety and nurtured by feelings of extreme vulnerability and a fragile self-confidence.

ONE MORE THOUGHT BEFORE MOVING ON

In this first part of the book, we began with a self-test to help you identify how controlling the Control Freak in your life actually is, and then we explored the top ten traits of most Control Freaks. We also examined the positive side of healthy control, and in this chapter we saw how anxiety fuels the behavior of Control Freaks. Now we are ready to roll up our sleeves and get to the part of the book that puts this preliminary understanding to work.

If you are like most people, wanting to improve your ability to cope more effectively with Control Freaks, I encourage you to review the book's table of contents and jump to the chapter in part 2 that focuses on the kind of relationship that gives you the most problems. For example, if you are a parent with a Tenacious Teen, move right to chapter 11. Or if you're married to a Supervising Spouse, read chapter 8 first. Each of the chapters in the next section of the book is designed to be read independently of any other. After you read the chapter that is most important to you, I encourage you to read the others in this section as well. But don't feel you need to read them in order. By the way, I also encourage you to read part 3 of the book, even if you feel you are not a Control Freak yourself. This final section can give you further

> To establish oneself in the world, one does all one can to seem established there already.
>
> FRANÇOIS, DUC DE LA ROCHEFOUCAULD

insight into the people you are coping with—and it may open your eyes to a blind spot or two where you can bring a healthier sense of balance to your relationships.

Now, if you are reading this book primarily because you want to control the Control Freak within *you*, I suggest you move right into part 3 of this book and begin reading the first chapter on diagnosing your Control Freak symptoms. The chapters in this section build on one another, so you will want to read each one in order. And if you do, I can assure you that soon you will be taming your controlling tendencies. You will begin making healthy choices to rebuild relationships that need attention, and you will learn to take charge without being a Control Freak. Once you have completed part 3, I encourage you to go back to part 2 and select a couple of chapters that may be especially pertinent to your life. Chances are you will learn more about yourself as you become more aware of other people's controlling tendencies too.

> To give up our pretensions is as blessed a relief as to have them gratified.
>
> WILLIAM JAMES

Whether you are trying to control the Control Freak in yourself or managing the Control Freaks around you, I wish you every success and pray that God will bless your journey.

PART 2

TAMING THE
CONTROL FREAKS
AROUND YOU

6

THE MEDDLING MANAGER

I have always believed that the best leader is the best server. And if you're a servant, by definition, you're not controlling.

HERB KELLEHER, CEO OF SOUTHWEST AIRLINES

One airline CEO was a master of the personal touch, spending hours with baggage handlers and pilots, getting to know his employees and their jobs; he persuaded them to accept pay cuts in return for an ownership stake. The concessions put the company—Western Airlines—so solidly in the black that the CEO was able to sell it to Delta for $860 million.

Another CEO, a certified Control Freak, meddled in everyone else's business. He berated people in front of other workers in an attempt to get them to do what he wanted. He also cut one-third of the workforce without warning and so embittered the survivors that his airline—Delta—lost its reputation for customer service and suffered an exodus of gifted managers who refused to work for such a Control Freak. The executive admitted he had devastated the workforce with his overcontrolling ways, and the board of directors, led by the former CEO of Western Airlines, forced him out.

Were these two high-level executives both financially savvy? You bet. They both had a proven track record of making lots of money for their companies. In any test of management principles, the two CEOs would have dueled to a draw. The difference was that one's leadership was fueled by high-octane anxiety and over-the-top control issues. We'll call him, and all of his ilk, a Meddling Manager.

The workplace is a natural breeding ground for controlling behavior. It is a place where productivity is prized and efficiency demanded. But these are the very qualities that can drive some subordinates straight to the hospital, literally.

How much latitude we have in our job or how much control we have in decisions about our work has a stronger influence on our health than high levels of stress. Rena Pasick, research associate at the University of California, Berkeley, views the question of job control as including how closely a person is supervised, how routine the work may be, and whether one's education or skills fit the complexity of the job.[1] The more control one has in one's work, the more likely a person is to enjoy it. Not only that, but the incidence of coronary heart disease is greater among employees who have less control.[2] When people sense they have little control over their work, they experience a rise in blood pressure and an increase in stress hormones.

> Surround yourself with the best people you can find, delegate authority, and don't interfere.
>
> RONALD REAGAN

Among employees, those with a stronger sense that they control what happens to them in life are less likely to become angry, depressed, or agitated when faced with conflicts on the job. But those who feel as if they have little control are more prone to getting upset or even quitting. And of all the relationships we have at work, the one with our boss or manager has the greatest impact on our well-being. Not only that, the biggest single complaint of American workers is poor communication with management; two-thirds say it prevents them from doing their best.[3]

DO YOU KNOW A MEDDLING MANAGER?

The following self-test can help you assess whether you are in a relationship with a Meddling Manager. Circle *Y* if the statement is true of the person you work for. Circle the *N* if the statement does not apply to this person.

Y   N   **1.** This person's management style is dictatorial and keeps people from taking risks.

Y   N   **2.** Most people would describe this person as a micromanager who wants to be more involved than is necessary.

Y   N   **3.** This person rarely delegates entire projects— only small pieces so he or she maintains ultimate control.

Y   N   **4.** While working for this person, I feel as if someone is looking over my shoulder every minute.

Y   N   **5.** Independent thought from a subordinate can be threatening to this person.

Y   N   **6.** This person hoards information.

Y   N   **7.** This person offends professionals by monitoring their morning arrivals, lunch hours, and evening departures.

Y   N   **8.** I sometimes feel as if I'm working for an overprotective parent.

Y   N   **9.** This person gives overexplicit directions on every project he or she "delegates."

Y   N   **10.** This person's management style discourages self-motivation and innovative thinking.

Scoring: Total the number of Ys you circled. If you circled five or more Ys, you are certainly in a relationship with a Meddling Manager.

WHY MANAGERS MEDDLE

In his book *Working with Emotional Intelligence,* Daniel
Goleman lists some of the most common and costly mistakes
of highly successful executives.[4] The people who were studied
ranged from department heads to CEOs. Their big mistakes
included setting unrealistic goals, striving for success at all
costs, being power hungry, driving others too hard,
being preoccupied with appearances, and needing
to be perfect. Sound like the makings for a happy
workplace? Hardly. But most of these successful
higher-ups got to where they are because of these
very qualities. No wonder so many underlings are forced to
contend with Meddling Managers. For some overcontrolling
managers, their "meddling" is what got them to the managerial
level to begin with.

> A man is known by the
> company he organizes.
>
> AMBROSE BIERCE

Few of us are willing to work with a boss who doesn't know
where to draw the line, at least not for very long. These are the
managers who not only set unrealistic goals for their group or
organization but are also unrealistic about what it takes to get jobs
done. They not only push other people too hard but also burn
them out. They micromanage to the point of madness.

Sure, it takes a degree of these qualities to be successful in
most businesses, but why do some managers not know when to
quit? Why do some managers qualify for full-blown meddlers?

The answer, more often than not, is that some managers
believe that no one else can do the job as well as they can. In
other words, these Meddling Managers fear failure. They have to
delegate (every "good" manager does), but deep inside they fear
someone else might make them look bad. "If you want it done
right, do it yourself" is their mantra. Underlying all their eager
efforts to be successful is a pool of anxiety that seeps down into
their managerial style and compels them to overcontrol. Let me
say it again—these managers have a dreadful fear of failure. This is
what fuels their compulsion to hold on to projects even after they

have "delegated" them. This is what keeps them from really letting go of the reins.

Henry, a manager of a successful consulting company, leaves nothing to chance. He hovers over his staff, providing exhaustive instructions on how to handle jobs they have done countless times before. On any given day, you might find Henry down in the mail room making certain that the mail is properly sorted. You might find him in the washroom making certain that Central Supply has bought the right soap. But you are most likely to find him going from desk to desk, monitoring everybody's phone calls, shaking his head, or writing a say-this note, or maybe drawing a finger across his throat if he decides the phone call is going badly.

> A cookie store is a bad idea. Besides, the market research reports say America likes crispy cookies, not soft and chewy cookies like you make.
>
> RESPONSE TO DEBBI FIELDS'S IDEA OF STARTING MRS. FIELDS COOKIES

The perfect workforce for Henry is not a team of competent men and women but dozens of cloned Henrys, each one of them thinking like, talking like, and writing like him. Only with clones could Henry overcome his reluctance to delegate. Only with robotic clones could Henry relax.

If we could get into Henry's head, we might hear him continually warning himself, "One slipup, and I could lose everything I've gained." In his effort to make very sure that there will be no slipups—ever—Henry, like every Meddling Manager, is compulsively driven to control.

This insight is vital to understanding the soul of every Meddling Manager. The more you realize how much your manager is trying to control his or her own anxiety by controlling you and everyone else, the more effectively you will be able to cope with his or her meddling ways.

COPING WITH A MEDDLING MANAGER

Nearly everyone who has been in the workforce long enough has worked for a Meddling Manager at some point. But not everyone knows how to handle this difficult relationship successfully. The following steps will help you regain control while dealing with your out-of-control supervisor.

Try On Your Manager's Shoes

The first step in getting along with any Control Freak, even your boss, is to see the world from his or her perspective. The more empathy you have for the person who irritates you the most, the less likely that person is to disturb you. Empathy is a powerful and fundamental interpersonal principle. Empathy begets understanding. And understanding begets patience. And patience begets lower levels of stress. Do yourself a favor and put yourself in your manager's shoes. Consider the worries you would have if you were in his or her place. Imagine what life must be like in his or her skin. How would you behave if your roles were reversed? What things might you do differently, and what things would you do just the same? Would some of your expectations for other people's work seem unrealistic to them but totally acceptable to you now that you are the person most responsible? The point in seeing things the way your Meddling Manager does is to help you relax a bit and not take his or her controlling behavior too personally. Remember that managers like yours live with a dreadful fear of failure that keeps them from fully delegating tasks. The more you keep this in mind, the easier the following steps will be for you to implement.

> Fragile and delicate are the feelings of most who seek our help. They need to sense we are there because we care . . . not just because it's our job.
>
> CHARLES R. SWINDOLL

Keep the Big Picture in Mind

César Ritz was a little perfectionistic. Let me rephrase that. César Ritz was a Meddling Manager with major Control Freak qualities. A few hours before the gala opening of his famous Ritz Hotel in Paris in 1898, he came into the dining room to check on the final preparations. Ritz sat down at a table and noticed at once that it was about two centimeters too high. He sat at another table. It also was two centimeters too high. So were a third and a fourth table. Ritz gave a few orders, and by eight o'clock the legs of all tables in the dining room had been shortened.

César Ritz's son Charles remembers that his father tried out every new mattress he ordered by sleeping one night on it. If the father didn't sleep well, he ordered that the mattress be returned.

I'll be the first to admit that working for César Ritz would not have been my idea of a good time. But after visiting his hotel in Paris nearly one hundred years after its grand opening, I can testify to his enduring care for treating his guests with outstanding quality. Do you think the world-famous Ritz Hotel would have the excellent reputation it does if it had not been for a major Meddling Manager? Probably not.

Of course, this does not mean we should put up with anything a Meddling Manager does as long as the end result is positive. Not by a long shot, and I'll have more to say about that shortly. But it does mean that it can be helpful to keep the big picture in mind when you are getting bogged down by your manager's controlling ways.

Meddling Managers like César Ritz are controlling, not only because of a fear of failure, but also because they care so deeply about what they do. Working with them can understandably try your patience, but keeping the big picture in mind can be helpful when your patience is near its end. Meddling Managers are usually very conscientious, dedicated, and hardworking. They take their work very seriously. Who can complain about these qualities?

> If a man does only what is required of him, he is a slave. If a man does more than is required of him, he is a free man.
>
> CHINESE PROVERB

I have a friend who works for a Meddling Manager at an advertising agency. His boss, the owner, has poured his life into this relatively small but very reputable company and cares deeply about keeping its positive reputation among clients. The boss cares so much that he often doesn't know how hard he is to work with. My friend, for example, has come close to quitting on several occasions because this man is such a micromanager. But after nearly a dozen years, my friend continues to work for this guy and seems to enjoy it more each year. Why? "Because my boss has such passion about helping our clients," my friend says. "And whenever I get frustrated with him, I remember that his meddling comes from wanting to do the very best job we can possibly do." Because my friend keeps the big picture in mind, he has come to appreciate his boss in spite of his controlling ways.

Demonstrate Your Competence

I counseled an employee who encountered a Meddling Manager on a new job. The new employee was an eager beaver, very competent. But his boss was sitting on every little thing. Whatever creative ideas the employee had were almost automatically squashed by his manager. The fellow's initial impulse was to say to the boss, "Hey, get off my back. That's what I was hired for. Let me be me." The more the man and I explored the repercussions of this kind of comment, the more open he became to exploring an alternative. "Give the boss a chance to see you dot all the i's and cross all the t's and get everything done," I counseled him. The idea behind my strategy was to give the micromanaging boss some time to lighten up by seeing that his new employee was not only competent but could also do exceptional work. The more the boss could see that the new employee would not let him down or do something flaky, the more he would come to trust this fellow's work style and ideas.

The same principle may apply to you. By putting up with your Meddling Manager's ways for a time, instead of fighting them, you may help him or her calm down and be less controlling. The fellow I was counseling did just that and discovered how much more pliable his uptight boss could become once he saw his new employee was open to suggestions and advice while he was proving his competence. My client learned to allay the fears of his boss by taking advice and earning his confidence. I remember the day he came into my office to report the good news that his controlling boss had checked up on him only once while he was implementing a project that he had initiated several weeks earlier. This was a huge turning point in my client's attitude toward his Meddling Manager.

Drown the Manager in Information

Think of Meddling Managers as overprotective parents. One of the best ways to help them relax is to keep them informed. The more you give, the less they have to worry and the more they'll let go. If you resist your boss's suggestion to hold a meeting with the people in Purchasing because you don't think it is a good use of your time, for example, he or she may assume you can't be trusted. The alarm will ring, and your boss may think, *This person is not a team player; this person won't take supervision; this person is trying to hide something.* Of course you are not trying to hide anything, but your boss doesn't know that— so tell him or her. Explain how you received the information you needed over the phone from Purchasing and think it is better to move forward without having a meeting. Better yet, after giving your boss this information, ask if he or she still thinks the meeting is necessary. Sure, you will feel as if you are asking the obvious, but providing Meddling Managers with constant information and inviting their input will make your relationship run more smoothly.

> Managers are maintainers, tending to rely on systems and controls. Leaders are innovators and creators who rely on people.
>
> JOHN C. MAXWELL

Dave learned this lesson while attempting to get out the word about a counseling center connected to a megachurch where he worked as an associate pastor. The executive pastor to whom Dave reported, a Meddling Manager for sure, had given him the assignment to do whatever he could to advertise that the church would be providing counseling services at reduced rates to meet the needs of people in the metropolitan community. One of the first things Dave did was to hold a luncheon for health-care professionals in the area and tell them about the church's new service. When the executive pastor learned of the luncheon after the fact, he went crazy. "Why didn't you tell me?" "How much did it cost us?" "How is it going to help us?" Dave was hit with a barrage of anxious questions because his Meddling Manager didn't completely trust him. And when Dave made his moves without keeping his manager informed, he created even more distrust. It didn't matter that he had good answers for his boss after the fact. The point was that his boss felt out of the loop and, like all Control Freaks, didn't like surprises (even good ones).

> The surest way to be deceived is to consider oneself cleverer than others.
>
> FRANÇOIS, DUC DE LA ROCHEFOUCAULD

This experience taught Dave the simple strategy of drowning his supervisor in information. For his next event, Dave sent his executive pastor E-mail and voice-mail messages about almost everything he did. He sent summary memos and meeting agendas. He ran brochure drafts by his boss and cleared any important dates by his calendar so his boss would have the option of attending if he wanted to. How long did Dave cater to his manager's controlling ways? Only through the next project. After that, Dave felt more and more trusted, appreciated, and supported by his boss. All because he put his boss at ease by drowning him in information.

Put It in Writing

One of the biggest frustrations people who work for Meddling Managers encounter is that these managers are rarely open to new ways of doing things, new methods or procedures. Say, for example, you have found an improved way for pulling data about past sales activity for year-end reports, but the Control Freak dismisses the idea out of hand. What can you do? You are convinced that computerizing the office records will save a tremendous amount of time, but the boss doesn't buy it. In a situation like this, the best thing to do is put the advantages of your idea in writing. Give your boss a chance to think about it. Don't confront the manager or ask to discuss it further. Provide lots of reasons why your way will be good. Overwhelm the manager with facts.

Why does this strategy work? Because it satisfies the Meddling Manager's underlying need for security. By providing this overcontrolling person with documented information, you are providing a security blanket to calm his or her anxiety. The more documented information you provide, the more secure the Meddling Manager feels and the more likely you are to get this person on board with your idea.

Going through the difficult exercise of gathering data to prove your point may not seem like the best use of your time, but it will be if you end up getting the desired outcome. Hard facts and information are the best tools for getting what you need from a controlling individual or, for that matter, a bureaucratic organization.

Understand the WADIT Principle

The U.S. standard railroad gauge (distance between rails) is 4 feet, 8½ inches. Why such an odd number? Because that's the way they built railroads in England, and American railroads were built by British expatriates. Why did the English adopt that particular gauge? Because the people who built the pre-railroad tramways used that gauge. They, in turn, were locked into that gauge because the people who built tramways used the same standards and tools they had used for building wagons, which were set on a gauge of 4 feet, 8½ inches. Why were wagons built to that scale? Because with any other size, the wheels did not match the old wheel ruts on the roads. So, who built these old, rutted roads? The first long-distance highways in Europe were built by Imperial Rome for the benefit of their legions. The roads have been in use ever since. The ruts were made by Roman war chariots. The width a chariot needed to be to accommodate the rear ends of two war horses was 4 feet, 8½ inches.

> Nothing is particularly hard if you divide it into small jobs.
>
> HENRY FORD

"That's the way *we always did it.*" Ever heard that one before? I call it the WADIT principle. And as the U.S. standard railroad gauge can attest, it's a pretty flimsy excuse. Nonetheless, most Meddling Managers swear by it. They often hold to their rigid rules and procedures as a way of containing their anxiety. It diminishes the possible failure rate. To try something new or different means taking a risk. And most Meddling Managers are risk averse, sticking to what they know.

If your manager adheres to the WADIT principle, carefully consider how you might propose a change to him or her. Rather than trying to get everything you want all at once, pace the process. In trying to change an office procedure, for example, you might do it more gradually so that the change is less threatening to your manager. Microchanges are always easier on micromanagers. Another effective way to handle the WADIT principle is to find other proven examples of what you are proposing to change. You might show your boss how a similar company implemented the plan you desire and how it improved the company's bottom line. The success of a similar company in doing something a certain way is often an effective way to get even the most entrenched Meddling Managers to reconsider their options.

Ask for More Autonomy

Do you find yourself debating the same issues over and over with your boss: how reports are approved and filed, the way your schedule is scheduled for you, and so on? When you identify a boomerang issue that continually smothers your independence, call a meeting with your boss and put it on the table. Let him or her know how having to get a standard report approved time and time again makes you feel. With calm composure, express your feelings about having to submit a schedule that is for no other purpose than to see how you are routinely using your time. If possible, show your boss how not having to do these sorts of things will actually increase your productivity and creativity on the job.

Judy, an entry-level reporter for a small-town newspaper, found herself under the supervision of a Meddling Manager who always wanted a complete rundown on every lead Judy was following for any particular story. This was okay with Judy in the beginning because she was learning the ins and outs of her job, but her boss's micromanaging soon grew wearisome. "It makes me feel like a child," Judy would tell her friends. Not wanting to rock the boat and be seen as a difficult person to work with, Judy felt uncomfortable asserting herself with her boss. It wasn't her nature to ask for what she wanted. But as she continued to lose countless hours of valuable work time because she was giving her boss repeated reports, she eventually made up her mind to say how she really felt. "I've been working at this job for nearly six months," she told her manager, "and although I still have much to learn, I think I'm doing pretty well." Her manager agreed. "But I feel I could be more productive if I didn't have to keep you informed of every potential lead I generate for a story. The amount of time I spend giving you these reports was valuable at first, but now I feel as if it is really slowing me down, and I wondered what you would think about my running with my investigations without giving you such detailed progress reports. Do you think we could try a different approach for a while and see what happens?"

> A manager may be tough and practical, squeezing out, while the going is good, the last ounce of profit and dividend, and may leave behind him an exhausted industry and a legacy of industrial hatred. I often wonder what strange cud such men sit chewing when their working days are over, and the accumulating riches of the mind have eluded them.
>
> ROBERT MENZIES

This meeting took all of Judy's courage, but it was one of the best things she ever did with her boss. Believe it or not, he was actually relieved to see her take more initiative and become less dependent on him. Not that he gave her free rein, but as a result of her request, he definitely lightened up.

The point is that if you are like Judy, you can ask for what you need to be a better worker. Propose a different strategy with your boss, something that is temporary, and see how it works. Sometimes it's as simple as that. Sure, there is always the possibility that your boss may put up a brick wall, but you won't know until you ask.

Know When It's Time to Move On

A study of some ten thousand American workers—including professors, lawyers, farmers, accountants, printers, librarians, sales and clerical personnel—concluded that people who are not happy with their jobs have a much higher risk of heart trouble.[5] The researchers characterized these workers as "striving without joy." Like Sisyphus, the character from Greek mythology, they feel condemned to push a heavy stone to the top of a hill only to have it always roll back down. That's the same dreadful feeling experienced by some workers who are overcontrolled by a Meddling Manager. If you try the interventions proposed in this chapter and give them adequate time to work but then still feel like this character from Greek mythology, you may need to consider moving on to another job in a totally new environment.

The amount of money a Meddling Manager at American Airlines saved the company in 1987 by eliminating one olive from each salad served in first class: $40,000.

Sometimes the only solution is to give in or leave. Corporations tend to self-select a certain kind of person to work for them. Overmanaging characterizes a lot of companies. Some people like to be given explicit instructions. If you don't, there may be a mismatch not only with your boss but with the organization as well. That's when it's time to move on.

You've read this chapter because you are trying to cope with a micromanaging boss who is probably driving you up the wall. I've done my best to give you practical strategies for improving your situation with him or her. Allow me to close by saying that if you put these strategies into action, you build a staircase leading to higher levels of potential fulfillment at work. As you become more and more fulfilled in what you do, you will find that your vocation becomes your avocation. You will find meaning and happiness in your work. In other words, once you improve your work situation with a micromanager, the drudgery and duty you feel right now will become pleasure and pride in a job well done. But if you sit back and do nothing about your situation except hope it will change, feelings of alienation and exhaustion will eventually move in. And as these feelings persist, you will burn out on work altogether. That's a high price you need not pay. Take courage, and then take action.

Your work provides the potential source of some of the most meaningful time you spend on this planet. You will "find satisfaction in [your] toilsome labor," says the writer of Ecclesiastes (5:18, NIV). Start today to make your job a better place to work tomorrow.

THE COERCIVE COLLEAGUE

Working for and with other people necessarily entails getting others to do what you want and dealing with others' efforts to get you to do what they want. This introduces a constant potential source of tension and battle of wills.

DEBORAH TANNEN

I have times when the day's writing assignment perfectly aligns with my personal life. As if for cosmic comic relief, it seems God sometimes provides circumstances that put me right in the middle of my writing assignment for a specific day. And today is one of those days.

I woke up to a phone call from a colleague who wanted to change an appointment. But this wasn't just any appointment. This was one we both had to wrestle with our calendars to get. Not only that, it required me to buy an airline ticket and travel more than a thousand miles to be there. I had guarded this time ferociously and put out the expense. Now he was telling me it was going to be "inconvenient" for him to make it.

"What do you mean, it's going to be inconvenient?" I asked. "I'm the one traveling across the country to attend this meeting."

"You're right," he admitted. "But since you are going to be here anyway, why don't you get together with Ted and work on the video project I've been telling you about?"

"I don't know what you're talking about. What video project?"

"You said you were on board with this. You can't back out now."

Suddenly *I* was the one backing out! And suddenly I felt roped in. Coerced. I began to wonder if this was part of the plan from the beginning. Had I been set up? Was this his way to get me into a project I didn't really know anything about?

My questions had no answers. Perhaps they never will. I don't know the end of this story yet. All I know is that I feel coerced by a colleague. And chances are you know this feeling too.

> Nothing makes a man so selfish as work.
>
> GEORGE BERNARD SHAW

Maybe you were asked by a coworker for some suggestions on a project. Because you take the assignment seriously, you present your ideas and make recommendations. Unbeknown to you, however, you have created the perfect environment for the Control Freak, who systematically and thoroughly dissects and dismisses each of your ideas until they become his or her own. In other words, the Control Freak tears apart your suggestions only to repackage them as thoughts that originated with him or her. You feel deflated and manipulated. You feel as if you've been had by a Coercive Colleague.

In this chapter I offer some of the most effective, proven techniques for coping with controlling coworkers. And believe me, I have good reason for knowing what works and what doesn't. We begin, however, with a brief assessment that will help you measure just how much you are being controlled by your colleagues.

DO YOU KNOW A COERCIVE COLLEAGUE?

The following self-test can help you assess whether you are in a relationship with a Coercive Colleague. Circle *Y* if the statement is true of the person you work with. Circle *N* if the statement does not apply to this person.

Y   N   **1.** I sometimes feel as if this person is looking over my shoulder at work.

Y   N   **2.** This person doesn't know the meaning of setting personal boundaries.

Y   N   **3.** This person can be pushy, directive, and sometimes even dominating on projects that aren't his or her complete responsibility.

Y   N   **4.** This person is known by others at work as being overbearing, strong-willed, and controlling.

Y   N   **5.** I sometimes feel guilty if I don't do something this person wants me to do.

Y   N   **6.** I sometimes feel like I am working *for*, rather than *with*, this person.

Y   N   **7.** I find myself second-guessing my performance around this person more than I do with other coworkers.

Y   N   **8.** This person is not only likely to take charge but also to take credit for a job well done or to shift blame when blame is found.

Y   N   **9.** I sometimes feel as if this person is sabotaging my effectiveness at work.

Y   N   **10.** I sometimes feel that this person manipulates me into doing things I don't want to do.

Scoring: Total the number of Ys you circled. If you circled five or more Ys, you are certainly in a relationship with a Coercive Colleague.

WHY COLLEAGUES COERCE

It's not enough for some Control Freaks to take charge at home; they want to hold the reins at work, too—even when they aren't the boss. The question is *why*. Isn't it enough to have battles of the will with spouses, parents, and children? Why are some colleagues dead set on controlling their peers as well as their partners?

Much of the answer is found in many of today's workplace trends. The urge to control coworkers, for example, can stem in part from the underlying anxiety that too often pervades the world of work these days. For example, a perceived lack of job security can add fuel to the Control Freak's fire. Let's face it, the word *downsizing* sends shivers through most employees these days. National and international companies have waged nerve-racking employment cutbacks on a major scale. Even more important is the fact that downsizing is here to stay. Thanks to the wizardry of the computer industry, qualified people are being laid off in shocking numbers. All this leaves some people scrambling to secure their place in the company's workforce. Their anxiety about keeping their job literally fuels their compulsion for control.

> Do thine own work, and know thyself, each of these two parts generally cover the whole duty of man, and each includes the other.
>
> PLATO

While many people face this perceived lack of job security today, Coercive Colleagues seem to experience it more deeply than others. Why? Because they already have an anxious predisposition that would be present even if they were in a relatively secure work position. Today's work environments, then, serve to amplify these people's insecurities and thus make them more controlling. Remember that all Control Freaks exhibit controlling behavior in an attempt to reduce their anxiety.

Another important factor contributing to colleagues' becoming more coercive today is that the workplace is requiring workers to be more educated and skilled than ever before. Ford

Motor Company says, "The quality goes in before the name goes on." For some assembly-line workers in Detroit, that slick slogan translates into "highly skilled but fewer employees" because assembly-line jobs are being taken over by sophisticated robots. And those who program the computers that activate these robots have skills gained through years of education and training. The people who guard the gates to union membership are looking for qualified people more than ever before. It's no wonder people who land a job they like often resort to controlling their coworkers. Right or wrong, they believe it might insure their job security—adding more fuel to the Control Freak fire.

> Work hard and become a leader; be lazy and become a slave.
>
> PROVERBS 12:24

Coercive Colleagues suffer from a low sense of competence or even from incompetence. To compensate, they resort to controlling behavior. In other words, they don't feel completely qualified or competent, so they begin playing a role that makes them seem more competent. And, in their opinion, that role calls for control of their colleagues. *If I'm giving advice and "overseeing" the work of my coworkers, I must be competent,* the unconscious reasoning of the Coercive Colleague goes.

Another reason colleagues resort to control is that the workplace is often a hotbed of hierarchy and ambition. Ask most people if they plan to still be doing what they're doing five years from now, and many will tell you they have their sights set on positions higher up. Unlike our parents and grandparents, few workers today stay with the same unchanging job. We are on the move. Climbing the proverbial ladder. And if you're going to climb the ladder, you may have to "control" those people who are reaching for the next rung—or so the thinking goes. Once again, we all experience competition from colleagues at work, but for the Coercive Colleague, this competition pushes a button of anxiety that cases them to fear failure. *If I don't get that promotion or that raise, I'll be a total loser,* they say to themselves. So they attempt to control you, their coworker, to increase their chances of personal success on the job.

To take this a step further, some controlling colleagues' level of insecurity and inadequacy runs so deep that they try to build themselves up by taking charge of people and projects that aren't their own. These are the power-hungry Control Freaks who are desperate to wield their influence on anyone they can. So they shift blame, withhold information, display their impatience, bark orders, or even sabotage projects to gain a fleeting sense of self-importance.

Whatever the reason for the controlling tendencies of coworkers, the bottom line is that they drive us nuts. So, we turn our attention to finding sanity in the sometimes crazy world of work.

COPING WITH A COERCIVE COLLEAGUE

Had enough of colleagues who don't know where they end and you begin? Tired of giving in to a coworker's push and pull? You're not alone. Over the years, experts have devised ways of coping with Control Freaks in the workplace, and here are some of their best suggestions.

Take a Good Look in the Mirror

The first step in coping with any difficult person is to recognize the part of yourself that is just like the person who's irritating you. Admittedly, that's not easy to swallow. After all, do you want to see yourself in someone like a controlling colleague? But this is some of the best advice you can get when it comes to coping. I've put it into practice many times myself—as recently as today. It wasn't easy. It was downright difficult. But I can truly tell you that it makes a significant difference. Once I took a moment to put myself in my colleague's shoes and see how I might do something very similar, I suddenly had more patience.

> Work is the meat of life, pleasure the dessert.
>
> B. C. FORBES

I began to regain my wits and even have a sense of humor about the situation. Understand that this is done for your benefit, not your colleague's. It is not a way of giving in to this person's manipulative way. Not by a long shot. This technique is designed to help *you* cope better. And it will.

Call on Other Colleagues for Help

A little reality check never hurt anyone—especially those of us trying to contend with a controlling colleague. That's why I suggest you enlist the help of a couple of coworkers who will shoot straight. Call on them for help by asking for their feedback on a specific situation where you've lost control. If you have an especially open and safe relationship with them, you may ask for their perception of this controlling colleague. What will you gain from this? For one thing, you may discover that others feel manipulated and controlled by this person too. And a little commiserating can go a long way—as long as it eventually leads to positive changes. The point is, a trusted colleague or two can help you see things as they really are and help you brainstorm about ways of improving your situation.

A word of caution is in order under this suggestion. As you call on trusted colleagues for help with your situation, they may begin to commiserate with you about the problem. And your commiserating, if you're not carefully guarded, can lead to gossip about the controlling colleague. And that will become more destructive than helpful. The Greek chronicler Hesiod, writing at the same time as Homer, declared near the end of *Works and Days:* "Gossip is mischievous, light and easy to raise, but grievous to bear and hard to get rid of." The apostle Paul warned about the destructive power of gossip and the condemnation that comes to gossips and busybodies who say things they shouldn't say

Blessed is he who has found his work; let him ask no other blessedness. He has a work, a life-purpose. He has found it and will follow it.

THOMAS CARLYLE

(1 Tim. 5:13). Gossip, no doubt about it, is evil. As you consult with supportive colleagues about taming your Control Freak colleague, take care to steer clear of it.

Coax Your Colleague with More Information

A little information can make almost everyone, Control Freak or not, feel more comfortable. Psychologists Ellen Langer and Susan Saegert tested the effects of information on women entering two supermarkets.[1] The women were given a long shopping list from which they were to select the most economical purchase in the store for each item. One group was told, "While you are carrying out the task, the store may become crowded. We know from previous research that crowding sometimes causes people to feel aroused and sometimes anxious. We just wanted you to know this so that if you feel anxious, you will know why." The other group did not get this information. Under crowded conditions, the informed group got more shopping items correct, were more satisfied with the store, and felt more comfortable than the "no-information" group did.

As this experiment so beautifully demonstrates, a little bit of information can make a world of difference in lowering our anxiety. Give it a try. Keep controlling coworkers informed. Let them know what's going on. If they are in the know, they may just drop their guard and become true peers. They may also come to believe that you, the person who keeps them up-to-date and informed, are the one person at work they can trust. It doesn't work with every controlling coworker, but it's worth a shot.

Greg, a sales rep in the high-tech industry, gave it a shot with a Coercive Colleague who continually pestered him with intrusive inquiries and unwanted advice. On a whim, Greg decided to make a game of trying to beat his colleague to the punch by giving him information before he asked. He called it the "radar routine." Soon after quarterly sales reports came out for each sales rep in his company, for example, Greg knew his nosy coworker would be asking him about his results, so Greg left him a voice-mail message telling his coworker exactly how he had done over the last few months. "Just thought you might be interested," he said at the end of his message. And he was right. His coworker shot back a reply: "Hey, thanks for keeping me in the loop, and congrats on a great quarter." The simple gesture was no skin off Greg's nose, and it seemed to do the trick for his Coercive Colleague. By dispensing a small bit of information to him from time to time, Greg noticed he wasn't nearly as controlling.

I admit that not all of us are made with the same good-natured disposition as Greg—I know some of you reading this are not about to give unnecessary information to a person who already drives you crazy—but if you can stand the thought of keeping your controlling coworker informed just a little bit more, I think you'll be amazed by the results. And remember, the goal is to make him or her feel less anxious. So if you are giving your coworker information with a chip on your shoulder, it will defeat the process entirely. The more you keep in mind the goal of lowering his or her anxiety level, the more successful you will be at diffusing controlling behavior.

> It is hard to master both life and work equally well.
>
> JOSEPH BRODSKY

Make Your Voice Heard

Some Control Freaks in the workplace are so influential and intimidating that it is difficult to ever set strong boundaries. Especially if you are a soft-spoken person, if you are an introvert, if you are short in stature, or if—I'm sorry to say—you are a female. Think about it. If you throw in the cultural and attitudinal deference often given to people with booming voices, to outgoing people, to tall people, and to males in the workplace—or to anything else that gives a coworker an edge over you—you just might feel like little David up against a Goliath of a colleague. If you identify with this, you may benefit from facing your controlling colleague on paper. While I don't recommend resorting to this as your only or even primary means of communication, I do believe there are times when your message may be best received through a memo or letter. If you come up with a solution that may get lost in a conversation with this person, for example, document it first and send a copy to other colleagues. This way you know your voice will be heard.

Subdue "The Talker"

We've all had the experience. You have an important meeting, time is limited, yet one of your colleagues in the group insists on taking valuable time to hear the sound of his or her own voice. You may be too polite to say it, but you and everyone else in the group know you have a controlling talker on your hands. By talking too much, this colleague dominates the meeting and controls the agenda. Well, before you resort to duct tape, consider some other remedies.

You might restrain the bigmouth by "removing" him or her from the meeting process by assigning that person to flip the flip chart or control the light switch at the back of the room. You might consider talking through him or her—the inappropriate sound of two voices vying for attention gets even the biggest bigmouth's attention. Of course, you do not want to be rude, you just want to set boundaries by giving clues to the talker. You might shift your position or avoid eye contact with the person and thereby avoid reinforcing the controlling behavior. Or you may simply ignore the talker. If this person is constantly raising a hand, don't look that way. If he or she interrupts, smile and say, "Let's look at that later."

I remember a time when I was asked to make a presentation to a small group of faculty at the university where I teach. I had prepared a few brief exercises to get people talking about the topic. What I hadn't prepared for was a colleague who

> But what is it good for?
>
> A CRITICAL ENGINEER AT THE ADVANCED COMPUTING SYSTEMS DIVISION OF IBM, 1968, COMMENTING ON THE MICROCHIP

wanted to dominate the conversation. Whatever someone else said, she either wanted to add to or take from it. Soon, it felt as if she, not I, was facilitating the meeting as well as the conversation. So, I avoided eye contact. That didn't stop her. She continued to blurt out her opinion without consideration of others. The quiet tension in the room was rising. I saw one fellow roll his eyes when she spoke. It gave me the courage to interrupt her: "Ellen, hold that thought. I want to know what others are thinking about this." You could almost hear a collective sigh of relief from the others. And the next time she started to dominate, another person picked up the job of reining her in. Without being rude, we got the message across.

By the way, it may become necessary to talk one-on-one with a Coercive Colleague who doesn't seem to get the message in a group context if you know you are going to run into the problem repeatedly. At the appropriate time, you can meet for coffee, perhaps, and ask that person how he or she thinks the meetings are going. You might also say something like, "You obviously have so much to contribute, but I wonder if you could ease up a bit so that those who aren't as confident as you feel comfortable getting their voices heard." If you approach it as a joint project that the two of you can work on, to get others talking as well, you may find your controlling colleague more supportive than you might imagine.

Turn Criticism into Constructive Change
During my graduate training to become a psychologist, I had a supervisor who loaned me a book titled *Control Theory* by William Glasser, founder of the Institute for Reality Therapy in Los Angeles. I'll never forget what that book taught me about criticism. "Nothing that we encounter leads to a greater and quicker loss of control than to be criticized," writes Glasser. "And, equally, it is harder to regain control when we are criticized than in any other situation." Then Dr. Glasser put the following sentence in

italics to underscore his main message: *"In my opinion, it is by far the single most destructive behavior we use as we attempt to control our lives."*[2]

If only your Coercive Colleague could hear and internalize such a message. Right? One of the Control Freak's favorite tools is criticism. He or she knows that a critical or negative word is a quick way for gaining control over people who don't know how to contend with criticism. "We tried that, and it didn't work" is the Coercive Colleague's theme song. When you find the controlling coworker in your life resorting to negative tactics, turn it around by asking: "How would you make it work this time?"

> Where the whole man is involved, there is no work. Work begins with the division of labor.
>
> MARSHALL McLUHAN

"How can we overcome those obstacles?" Chances are, this person is used to shutting down a good brainstorming session with criticism. By getting him or her to be more constructive, you regain the control you might otherwise have relinquished.

I have a friend who works at a well-known nursery in Seattle. He is a gentle, soft-spoken horticulturist with advanced training who really knows his stuff, especially when it comes to fruit trees. But one of his fellow workers, who has neither the expertise nor the gentle spirit he has, persists in criticizing my friend's work. "That plant will never be productive growing up that trellis without more light," he will say. Or, "Those bushes you just planted are way too close to each other to be of any good when they get bigger." My friend asked me for advice on taming his controlling colleague, and when he took my suggestion not to allow this guy to get away with a criticism without offering a solution, the number of criticisms dropped off drastically. "When Harry would criticize my work, I used to get so defensive, it made my blood boil," my friend told me. "Now, Harry knows that if he critiques my work, I'm going to ask him to offer constructive advice, so he doesn't dish out his critical comments nearly as often." My friend went on to tell me that he

doesn't always take Harry's advice too seriously either. "Sometimes he actually has a good idea," he says, "but most of the
time I smile and say thanks without changing a thing. It's made
working with Harry so much easier."

Don't Be Afraid to Confront Your Colleague

To Roger Mosvick, author of *We've Got to Start Meeting Like This*,
the imbalance between shy people and demonstrative people is
a major problem in the workplace. To keep from being steam-
rollered by a hard-driving colleague or a Machiavel-
lian manipulator, we have to be willing to take a
stand, set some boundaries, and confront our
colleague. Of course, this can be excruciating for
some people who are especially reserved. If that's
your case, let me make a few suggestions.

> Work and play are an
> artificial pair of opposites
> because the best kind of
> play contains an element
> of work, and the most
> productive kind of work
> must include something
> of the spirit of play.
>
> SYDNEY J. HARRIS

First, clarify what you want. You need to be
certain of your desired outcome when confronting
another person. The more specific you are with this,
the better. Rather than saying to yourself that you
don't want this person to bug you anymore, think through in
specific terms what behaviors bug you the most. Perhaps you
don't want this person touching papers on your desk, for example.
Or maybe you don't want this person calling you at home after
hours about work-related matters. The point is to be specific so
that you know exactly what you are going to confront the person
about.

Next, set a time and a place to meet with the person,
choosing a place where you are likely to feel confident. Then
begin the time by giving this person any genuine compliments
you can. This will make him or her more likely to hear your
concerns and thus increase the chances of a positive outcome.
Once you have done this, look directly at the person, maintain
an open posture, and literally "stand your ground" by not physically backing away. Then present your concern as politely and

concisely and directly as possible. It is helpful if you can express your concern in terms of how you are feeling and what you are wanting. Rather than accusing your colleague of something, state your feelings: "I need you to know that it is disconcerting to me when you go through documents on my desk. I consider that my private space and would really appreciate it if you would respect that. What do you think?" What you do next is very important. Maintain your open posture and direct eye contact. Then, be quiet. Don't speak. Allow your coworker to respond before you say anything else. This puts the ball squarely on his or her side of the court.

Being assertive takes courage. If you are still feeling as if you couldn't confront your Coercive Colleague, try talking to supportive friends who might even help you role-play the scenario. If this doesn't help and you become anxious just thinking about something like this, I strongly urge you to consider getting some assertiveness training from a qualified psychologist. A couple of sessions with a trained professional may make all the difference in your getting the respect you deserve from a controlling colleague—as well as the rest of the people in your workplace.

Know When the Line Has Been Crossed

Almost anyone can put up with a few controlling tendencies here and there. It's a part of human relationships, both at home and at work. But in some work settings with some people, the controlling goes too far. Way too far. Know this: controlling coworkers can cross the line. That happens anytime you feel threatened, set up, in danger, or abused. Sadly, there are some Control Freaks who may actually try to get you fired with their controlling ways. This is obviously inexcusable and must be noted and reported. If you have a pattern of being manipulated and betrayed by coworkers who are trying to undercut you, don't sit back and take it. Follow your workplace procedure for

> We are, each of us, angels with only one wing. And we can only fly embracing each other.
>
> LUCIANO DE CRESENZO

reporting such incidents immediately. Don't allow your neck to be used for them to sharpen their ax on.

The goal of all these strategies is to regain control of your work environment and stand on a level platform with your colleagues—in order to get your work accomplished. You are no good to your company or your coworkers if you feel you are being badgered or belittled by someone you work with. So, take a stand. Don't let another workday go by without putting these strategies to the test.

8

THE SUPERVISING SPOUSE

It is almost impossible in our times to think about love, sex, intimacy, or marriage without thinking about power.

MICHAEL VINCENT MILLER

You think it's invigorating to keep the house at fifty-nine degrees, while your spouse shivers beneath layers of fleece. Every night you go through the same routine—you turn the thermostat down, she turns it up, repeatedly.

The struggle for control of the thermostat is only one of countless fields in which couples battle for control. The roasting pan could rot in the sink for days in some homes because neither partner will give in and wash it. And determining whose turn it is to choose which video to rent can quickly escalate into a screaming match for some out-of-control couples. Then there are those Supervising Spouses who are supercontrollers, prescribing to their partner what he or she should wear, read, and do—mapping out his or her entire life.

I don't know where you and your partner stand on the Control Freak continuum, but since you're reading this chapter, you probably have one question in mind. And it's the same one I received in a letter shortly after my book *High-Maintenance Relationships* was released. Here's part of what this reader wrote:

My spouse and I have been married for nearly a dozen years, and compared to most married couples, we seem to have a pretty good relationship. No infidelity, no drug or alcohol use, no financial problems.

But there is something about my husband that is as irritating as a fly that keeps buzzing around your head. He can't let go of the details. He worries, frets, and stews about the tiniest of things. He makes both of us miserable when things don't go exactly the way he thinks they should. And that's most of the time.

It's gotten so bad, I asked our minister to talk to him. He did. And he told me my husband is a Control Freak. The minister also said I'm going to have to live with this problem since my husband probably won't change. Is that true? Can a Control Freak ever change?

I've heard that question countless times—most often from a discouraged spouse. Sure, we would all like our Meddling Manager or Coercive Colleague to lighten things up at work. And yes, we would love to see things change with a pushy parent or in-law. But when it comes to our marriage, our life partner, most of us are especially invested in making things right. After all, we're talking about our soul mate, the one person we have vowed to love forever. No wonder we are desperate to know if he or she can change.

As I told this reader and everyone else who has asked me this question over the years: Yes! It is possible for a controlling spouse to change—but not overnight. It takes time and requires work. In fact, at times you may feel as if you are doing more of the work than your partner. But if you hang in there, you will reap the kinds of remarkable rewards only married couples can enjoy. And this chapter will show you how.

DO YOU KNOW A SUPERVISING SPOUSE?

The following self-test can help you assess whether you are in a relationship with a Supervising Spouse. Circle *Y* if the statement is true of your spouse. Circle *N* if the statement does not apply.

Y   N   **1.** Most people who know my spouse well feel that he or she doesn't like to give up control.

Y   N   **2.** My spouse can throw a tantrum in order to get his or her own way.

Y   N   **3.** My spouse spends an inordinate amount of time organizing and planning, getting everything just the way he or she likes it.

Y   N   **4.** I sometimes feel as if my partner is planning my entire life.

Y   N   **5.** Power struggles have become commonplace in our marriage.

Y   N   **6.** Sometimes I feel my self-confidence draining because my spouse thinks I'm doing things the wrong way.

Y   N   **7.** My spouse controls (or wants to control) almost all the family finances.

Y   N   **8.** If it were up to my spouse, he or she would make all the decisions.

Y   N   **9.** My partner wastes no time in pointing out what's wrong or what he or she needs me to do.

Y   N   **10.** My spouse doesn't know the meaning of the words *equal* or *joint decision.*

Scoring: Total the number of Ys you circled. If you circled five or more Ys, you are certainly in a relationship with a Supervising Spouse.

WHY SPOUSES SUPERVISE

We have some good friends, a husband and wife, who live in Kansas City. Not long ago we were talking about a recent trip they took to Florida. Kevin told me, with some measure of excitement, that thousands of people are clamoring for the opportunity to live in a highly controlled environment called Celebration, Florida, a Disney-designed real-life town. It's a high-tech neighborhood in which a digital network links each resident to a central monitoring point that records comings and goings. But that's not the controlling part. The inhabitants of this community agree to live by a long list of rules and regulations that surely were written by a committee of Control Freaks: Residents will be punished for having more than one garage sale a year; residents cannot park more than two cars in front of their house at any given time; lawns must be manicured weekly; no RVs are allowed to enter the neighborhood; and on and on.

While Kevin was somewhat intrigued by the concept, Kathy, his wife, was appalled. "Give me a break," she said over dinner with us. "I don't want my neighbors dictating what I can and can't do with the property I own. I already get enough of that from Kevin." We laughed and all agreed that she was right. And Kevin, a self-confessed Control Freak, agreed that he sometimes overcontrols his home and his spouse.

The question every partner married to a Supervising Spouse has is *why?* Why does he or she have to be in charge? Why does my husband have to control all the money decisions? Why does my wife have to be so fussy about what I do with my dirty clothes? Why, why, why?

The answer is obvious to any Control Freak. Home is the one place we can—or think we can—do anything we want. It's the one place where we have "total control." If you think controlling tendencies can get out of control at work, you haven't seen anything until you see a Control Freak loose in a house.

Some people are even cashing in on this compulsion. "We're selling the perception of control," commented the vice president of Hold Everything. He was describing the philosophy behind his store's upscale mail-order catalog and retail outlets dedicated to home organization. "I see organization as controlling your space," he explained. "We're in charge of our workplace, and if all of a sudden we go home and can't find our shoes, we're no longer in control of our lives."[1] Of course, his store can sell you something to organize your shoes and thus "regain control of your life." So the Control Freak hands over the credit card.

Of course, controlling how one organizes a closet or kitchen drawer is one thing, but controlling a person is quite another. That's where true Control Freaks run into serious problems in marriage. So, if this is the kind of Supervising Spouse you're contending with, the kind that wants to control things not only in the house but also in you, let me remind you what is driving his or her behavior. The husband who tries to prevent his wife from going out with her female friends on a Friday evening, or the wife who tries to change her husband's career objectives into something he doesn't desire is reacting out of deep-seated anxiety. These spouses fear losing control of time, of money, or of the person they love the most. So, in a desperate attempt to maintain control, they try to control their partner all the more.

> Selfishness is not living as one wishes to live, it is asking others to live as one wishes to live.
>
> OSCAR WILDE

Another way of looking at this underlying cause of control is to think about it in terms of security. Supervising Spouses, more than most marriage partners, are reacting to perceived threats of all kinds. An action by their spouse may threaten their freedom, their sexuality, or their identity. A husband, for example, who gets bent out of shape because his wife is going out with her female friends instead of him on a Friday evening may feel that her decision threatens his influence in her life. He may feel that the message is that he's not as important to her. He may simply feel that his control over his time is being threatened. The weekend he was hoping for isn't going to happen because she is taking his control. *If she is doing this now, what else is she going to be doing without my say?* he asks himself. *If she chooses her other friends over me, where do I stand in this relationship?* This kind of thinking fuels more anxiety, which leads to more control.

Marriage exacerbates controlling tendencies. Think about it. Many of us believe love means the other person should put us first and be devoted to making us happy. This seems perfectly logical, so the Control Freak wife digs in her heels when decisions come up, just to test her husband's devotion. She mentions going out for dinner, but he says he wants to stay home—and she feels her anger rise. *Doesn't what she wants count for anything? Is he taking this relationship for granted?* Suddenly, she really, really wants to go out. When she first brought it up, she was merely thinking about shrimp scampi—now he's got to give in to her as proof that he loves her. Too many controlling couples put one another through this kind of love test, and many don't even realize they're doing it.

> Chains do not hold a marriage together. It is threads, hundreds of tiny threads that sew people together through the years.
>
> SIMONE SIGNORET

In addition to anxiety, there is another reason some spouses try to control each other more than they should. It's a power trip for some. A couple I know is a prime example. You would not believe the transformation this new wife has gone through in the few years they've been married. She used to be a happy-go-lucky young woman with a beautiful tangled head of curls and a whimsical way of dressing. Today you are more likely to see her with carefully coiffed hair and a sophisticated beige cashmere suit. When I asked her about the drastic change, she quickly replied, "Ken likes to say I'm his creation." I bet he does. Think of the power that comes from "creating" your own spouse. And think of the dysfunction.

Every relationship has areas in which one person leads and the other follows. That's okay. It's even healthy. But when a Supervising Spouse has to be in control constantly to feel secure, when he or she spends an inordinate amount of energy trying to hold on to the reins of power, it's time to get serious. It's time to intervene.

COPING WITH A SUPERVISING SPOUSE

Spouses plagued by a dominant partner run the risk of not only an unhealthy marriage but also an unhealthy body. And now a study has documented just how bad controlling behaviors can be. Researchers at the University of Utah have found that people whose spouses are particularly controlling experience blood pressure hikes that may raise their risk of heart disease.[2] If you needed another reason, that should supply a booster in your motivation to cope with a controlling partner. Here are a few proven techniques for doing just that.

Take an Honest Look at Yourself

I mention this first because it is so crucial to every marriage. Too often in a marriage relationship, both people insist that the other always wants to be in control. Each cites areas in which the other insists on taking over. Maybe in your case it's true. Maybe it is all one-sided, and your partner is totally to blame. But if so, you would be the first couple like that I've met. Every marriage therapist will tell you that marital problems are never all on one side or the other. Before you label your partner as the mold from which all other Control Freaks were cast, pause for a few minutes to recall what and how you may have contributed to the state of your Supervising Spouse.

> A good marriage is not one where perfection reigns: It is a relationship where a healthy perspective overlooks a multitude of "unresolvables."
>
> JAMES C. DOBSON

Not long ago I asked my wife, Leslie, to make a list of things that would make me a better husband. I really did. We were speaking at a marriage conference at which one of the other speakers tossed out this idea, and it sounded interesting to me. Well, Leslie had no problem creating her list. I joked with her about how easy this was for her to do and how long her list became. But as we talked together about the things she had noted, she began to reflect on how she was contributing to some of the negative things I was doing. One of her items, for example, said, "I would like you to involve me more in some of your decisions that have an impact on our family calendar." As she read this off her list, she paused and then said, "As I'm thinking about this one, I know that you used to ask for my input more than you do now, and that's probably because before we had our baby, it didn't really matter as much to me." In other words, Leslie was taking part ownership in one of the controlling things I do.

I can't begin to tell you how much easier it was to hear Leslie's critique when she took partial responsibility for the situation. It's that kind of honest self-examination that I'm talking about in this first step. I'm not asking you to make excuses for your partner's bad behavior. I'm just suggesting that you own whatever it is that you may have contributed to the control issues. By taking some of the responsibility, you will make it easier on yourself as you put into practice the steps that follow.

Put the Problem on the Table

This may sound like an obvious step to some people, but not to others. I've counseled plenty of people who think they are being loving by not bringing up problems to their partner. Well, as noble as that tactic might seem, it's not. If a marriage is ever going to reach the level of health and well-being you dream of, it will be because you honestly face friction between the two of you. So put the problem out there. Talk to your spouse about your feelings and perceptions. Gently say something like, "I know you want what's best for our relationship, but sometimes I feel as if I'm only the passenger, as if my voice doesn't count." Then follow it up with some specific recent examples that will make your point clear. Here's a possible scenario:

Gina to her Supervising Spouse, Bill: I really appreciate the

expertise you bring to our family finances, but I need to talk to
you about something.

Bill: What's wrong?

Gina: Nothing's wrong. I just want to tell you how I'm feeling about some of our recent money decisions.

Bill: Oh boy, is this one of those conversations
sparked by a self-test you took in the waiting room of
our doctor's office while reading one of those
women's magazines?

> A happy marriage is the union of two good forgivers.
>
> ROBERT QUILLEN

Gina: Bill, I'm serious. I really do appreciate
how well you manage our money, but recently I've been feeling
that you make decisions about saving and spending, but you don't
really involve me.

Bill: Do you want a bigger allowance?

Gina: That's just it. I don't want an allowance.

Bill: What? That'd be fine with me.

Gina: No. You're missing the point. When you give me an
"allowance," I feel as if I'm twelve years old. I feel like a kid, not a
partner. Last week I wanted to buy a gift for Barbara, and I didn't
have enough money, so I waited until Monday when you gave me
my week's worth of money.

Bill: I work hard for our money, Gina. Maybe you—

Gina: I know you do. But that's not the point. I want to feel
more like a team in our money decisions. I don't need to spend
more money, but I don't like having to ask you every time I need
to buy something. I just want to be active in our financial decisions.

Bill: Do you want to pay the bills? set up the budget? write
all the checks?

Gina: I don't know. Maybe. I want to do anything I can to
help, but most of all I want to be more together with you on this.
We don't have to make any specific decisions right now. I'm just
telling you how I feel.

Bill: That's it?

Gina: Well, yes. Since I've never really said anything about how you manage our money and since these feelings have been building up in me recently, I just wanted you to know that I'd like to play a more active role in all of this.

Bill: Well, have you ever seen the family finances spreadsheet I worked out on the computer? It's really cool. Let me get my laptop.

This interaction that Gina initiated could have gone a hundred different directions, but she kept working with her Supervising Spouse to get the problem out on the table. Although he had a tough time hearing it at first, Bill eventually received the message. That's the goal of this step.

Look for Solutions Instead of Pointing Your Finger

This may be common relationship advice, but it's often forgotten. And it's too good to neglect. Think about the struggle to control the thermostat, for example. It's easy to point one's finger and accuse your partner of thinking only of himself or herself. But maybe the problem could be derailed if the chilly spouse could simply rely on a space heater to warm a small area, maybe the TV room or the home office, while the heartier partner roams in the cooler rest of the house. In the bedroom and under the covers, try dual-control electric blankets to accommodate your different needs for heat or coolness. The point is that you can save your marriage a lot of tension by simply working on solutions instead of trying to lay blame.

> Let the wife make her husband glad to come home, and let him make her sorry to see him leave.
>
> Martin Luther

Sheila was a Supervising Spouse who didn't want her husband, Del, working out at the gym three evenings a week. Del, on the other hand, really enjoyed this time and looked forward to venting some of his work frustration before coming home by stopping off at the gym to lift weights. One evening Sheila put her foot down. "If you keep going to that gym," she told Del, "you might as well plan on sleeping on the couch." He couldn't believe his ears. "I don't want a husband who gives away half his free time to something that doesn't matter," Sheila continued.

Del knew she was steaming and fought the urge to get defensive and lay blame. He took a deep breath and said, "Honey, I can tell this really upsets you, and I can see why you're frustrated, but let's consider some other options."

When Sheila cooled down, they took a walk around their neighborhood and talked more about their needs. Sheila came to understand that working out really helped Del reduce his stress, and Del realized that Sheila was feeling cheated out of family time with him. After each of them felt completely understood, they worked toward a solution and came up with several options. One, they could buy some weights for Del to lift at home. Two, they could go to the gym as a family one or two nights a week. Three, Del could make his trip to the gym on his lunch hour during the middle of the day. In the end, they did a combination of these things, and that particular problem was solved.

Whatever your specific situation with your Supervising Spouse, do your best to put on your thinking cap and think of creative solutions to make you and your partner happy.

Pinpoint What Matters Most

In a sense, marriage is easier when you both don't care as much about the same things. Otherwise, you find yourselves battling about everything from how to cut carrots to how to make the bed. Do yourself a favor and identify those things that matter most to you. This will help you keep from turning every decision into a power struggle. It will keep you from fighting simply to win and will help you focus on the things you truly care about.

> The day I finally realized I didn't need to control my wife . . . and that if I did, I would destroy our marriage—was the day our marriage began.
>
> GERRY SPENSE

In our own marriage, Leslie and I made lists of little things that mattered to each of us individually. I'm embarrassed to say that my list was much longer than Leslie's. As the more controlling partner, however, I guess I shouldn't be surprised. Leslie wasn't. She laughed about some of my items, but in the end the list helped both of us clarify the things that really mattered so that she would know what pushed my Control Freak buttons. I have a favorite towel I like when I come out of the shower, for example. When Leslie uses it to dry off our baby after his bath, that means I won't get that towel in the morning. Until I put this on my list, Leslie didn't know it really mattered to me. These kinds of things may seem pretty small, but sometimes the small stuff is what Control Freaks sweat the most.

Keep Score

One way to break the cycle of control is to keep score. I don't mean the kind of mental scorekeeping in which so many of us secretly engage, tallying everything we give and waiting to see if we get it back. I mean doing it openly, making a written note of who won each time a decision is made, even if it's just which television program to watch. I know, this sounds embarrassingly petty. But for couples who are really struggling to balance the power in the relationship, this exercise is one of the most effective methods I have used in my marriage-counseling practice. It's as simple as it sounds. For a day simply keep track of who makes what decisions. Many times you'll be tempted to say, "It was mutual." But force yourself to choose, and give the point to the person who took the lead. If you both agree on going to the deli for lunch, for example, give the point to the person who made the suggestion. Whoever pays the credit-card bill gets a point for taking the lead there. The person who determines the order in which errands are run when you're both in the car also earns a point. So does the person who decides to drive, and so on.

The point of this seemingly silly exercise is to get both of you aware of what you are already doing. By "keeping score," both of you are forced to raise your awareness of how the power is balanced (or out of balance) in your relationship. The results may surprise you. And, by the way, most couples who have tried this can barely hold out for a day. So don't try to do this much longer than that. A mere twenty-four hours (especially on a weekend) will reveal more than you probably care to know.

> The curse which lies upon marriage is that too often the individuals are joined in their weakness rather than in their strength—each asking from the other instead of finding pleasure in giving.
>
> SIMONE DE BEAUVOIR

This exercise has several positive outcomes: It puts your power struggle on the table, and that can drain a lot of emotional poison. It also helps you and your spouse become more aware of the balance of power in the relationship and recognize which arenas each of you controls. You may always feel like the loser because your spouse often gets his or her way about social plans and spending. But this may be balanced by your frequent victories in scheduling, parenting, and vacation planning. Whatever you learn through this exercise, it will set you up nicely for the next step in taming your Supervising Spouse.

Negotiate Your Role

Whether or not you keep score, it's important for a couple to decide together who is best at certain tasks and who should control them. If you are a better cook, you should be in control of the kitchen, and your spouse needs to agree to stay clear. If your spouse is better behind the wheel, he or she should drive the car. The trick to making this strategy work is reminding a Control Freak of your agreement. If your partner starts telling you how to cut carrots, for example, say, "We agreed that this is my domain, and I am in control here." Maybe such delegated roles seem too formal and prescribed for you. I agree, they can be. But negotiating your assigned roles can ease your life with a Supervising Spouse and help him or her back off.

This simple strategy can be a true turning point for many people trying to tame their Control Freak spouse. I want to underscore how this works. Consider Joan and Craig. Food preparation was a special concern to this couple. Most of their fights started in the kitchen. Why? Because they both cared about how their meals were planned and prepared. They took pride in growing many of their own vegetables and eating meals made from scratch. There were no frozen dinners in this home. Meals were occasions to celebrate, and they enjoyed a fully equipped gourmet kitchen in which to prepare them. At least they tried to enjoy it. More often than not, their meals were spoiled because Joan had to take charge of the whole works. Joan was the self-confessed Control Freak in the relationship. And for nearly fourteen years of marriage, Craig had tried to be the loving spouse by letting Joan run the show. But he became weary. He sometimes felt as if his ideas and opinions didn't even matter, not to mention his own giftedness in the kitchen.

> A marriage is like a long trip in a tiny rowboat: If one passenger starts to rock the boat, the other has to steady it; otherwise they will go to the bottom together.
>
> DAVID ROBERT REUBEN

Here's what they did to overcome the problem and build a better marriage: They sat down at their kitchen table with a pad of paper and a couple of pens and discussed what each of them thought the other person's strengths were. They each made a list on their own. They also made a list of the things they thought they personally were good at and then compared notes. They were surprised to discover the things the other person appreciated about them as well as how similar their lists were.

This process set them up for deciding what areas in their life they could more or less leave to the other person. In the kitchen, their prime problem spot, Craig always prepared their outdoor dinners and put up with a lot of criticism from Joan in the process. But both of them agreed that Joan is actually better at making a tangy barbecue sauce and cooking meat on the grill. Craig, on the other hand, has a flair for salads. They each agreed that these would then become their personal domains. No critical comments from the other person were allowed unless requested.

You can do the same thing with your partner. Whenever you find yourself in arenas that trigger control issues, have a meeting to discuss your strengths in that area and agree on your respective domains. Then, the next time your Control Freak steps in to offer unwanted advice or direction, you can remind him or her of your agreement. Give this a shot. It really can make a world of difference in living with a Supervising Spouse.

Learn to Fight Fair

In a study published in the *Annals of Behavioral Medicine*, researchers studied forty-five young couples, some of whom included Control Freaks. The researchers hooked up the spouses to blood-pressure monitors and asked them to argue opposing positions on a given topic. Results showed that arguing with a partner who was perceived as dominant and controlling was associated with larger increases in blood pressure than arguing with a spouse considered to be more objective and less pushy. What's more, couples who learned how to argue more fairly showed much smaller increases in blood-pressure hikes.

One of the most important traits of couples who fight fair is the focus they put on the problem, not the person. I don't know of a single person who has ever changed a spouse through arguing. Our natural impulse during conflict is to defend and protect our position, not to accommodate the other person, even when it's our spouse. If you accuse your spouse of always making you late, he or she is probably not going to say, "Oh, you're right. I'll be different from now on." Your spouse is more likely to tell you that you only make it worse by pressuring him or her or that you are too impatient or that you are at fault for a hundred other reasons. You will be far more productive if you focus on the problem of being late and work together as a team to devise a way of avoiding it. In other words, separate the problem from your partner.

> This explains why a man leaves his father and mother and is joined to his wife, and the two are united into one.
>
> GENESIS 2:24

Fair fighting also means learning not to demean or belittle the other person's opinions. It means not attributing malicious intent to your partner. It means learning to express your own feelings clearly and effectively and to express an understanding of your partner's point of view. Fighting fair hinges on two people's willingness to flex and yield to one another. It has to do with two people who are trying to achieve peace, not to prove their points. I think that's what is meant in the Bible where it says, "Wisdom . . . is peace-loving and courteous." It goes on to say, "It allows discussion and is willing to yield to others; it is full of mercy and good deeds" (James 3:17, TLB). So, learn to fight fair. It just may be the best tool you have in controlling your Supervising Spouse.

Hand Over the Reins When You Can

You can sometimes stop a Supervising Spouse right in his or her tracks by handing over the reins. I'll never forget the time I was in the passenger seat and my wife was driving our brand-new car for the first time. Because I was so anxious about protecting this new machine, I was hypervigilant with my suggestions. "Don't drive so close to the parked cars over here," I'd say. "You see that red light, don't you?" After a few minutes of this, Leslie pulled off to the side of the road, unbuckled her seat belt, stepped out of the car, and gave the wheel over to me. Suddenly I saw my controlling ways replayed in living color. And I felt like a heel.

> The capacity to care gives life its deepest significance.
>
> PABLO CASALS

Nothing she could have said would have been more powerful than what she did. I immediately knew I was wrong and wanted to take it all back. In fact, I tried. "I'm sorry," I pleaded. "Go ahead and drive. I'm being a jerk, and I know it." Leslie refused. She waited until I got out of the car and took over the wheel. I learned my lesson that day. And it stuck. I don't think I've made a critical comment or given her unwanted advice on her driving ever since.

You can use the same strategy with your Supervising Spouse. If your partner is telling you how to organize the garage or clean the kitchen floor, let him or her do it. Hand the broom over with a smile. "If you're not happy with the way I'm doing this," you might say, "I'll gladly let you do it." Your spouse will get the message. And if he or she doesn't, it's one less task on your to-do list.

Refuse to Play the Blame Game

Have you noticed lately that everyone seems to be a victim? The media has. The *New Yorker* magazine, for example, recently featured a cover story with the title "The New Culture of Victimization," and the headline of the inside story was "Don't Blame Me!" On the cover of a recent *Time* magazine, these words appeared: "Cry Babies and Eternal Victims!" *Esquire* followed with an article titled "A Confederacy of Complainers." It seems people these days don't want to be held accountable. I'll leave it to social commentators to explain just how our new culture of victimization will affect society, but I know exactly how it can affect a marriage.

Once a husband or wife becomes wrapped up in the blame game, a vicious cycle of shirked responsibility permeates the relationship. That's why even though you may live with a Control Freak, it is important not to play the victim. You don't have to live this way. You have the power to change the dynamics of the relationship. My final suggestion in this chapter is more of a challenge: Take responsibility for the relationship, and refuse to play the blame game.

Just how do you do this? By making a decision. It comes down to your will and the capacity you have to say, "I'm not going to whine about a situation and act as if I can do nothing to improve it." It is a decision you will have to make a million times. Each time you are tempted to throw a pity party because you are married to a Control Freak, you will have to make the decision again. Remember, you can blame your partner all you want, but it will do absolutely nothing to improve your relationship. So, why bother? Instead of playing the blame game, spend your time and

energy taking constructive actions to make your marriage everything it was ever meant to be. And along these lines, let me just
remind you that marriage was never meant to be lived "happily
ever after." That is a fairy-tale fantasy that has poisoned too many
marriages. We all hit tough spots. The difference between couples
who wallow in them and those who rise above them is found in
their capacity to adjust their attitude in spite of their circumstances.

Chances are that just this week you and your partner had a situation that required negotiation and compromise—a money matter
came up, a conflict in household chores arose, or a discrepancy
over discretionary time raised its head. And chances are, you eventually worked out a compromise or a solution. But if you didn't, if
there is an area that continues to be a stubborn problem, you may
want to get some outside help. It never feels good to ask someone
else for help. But seeking counsel is never a sign of weakness. In
fact, it just may be your ticket out of an overly controlled home
front and into the marriage you've long imagined.

9

THE PUSHY PARENT

A lot of people go through life beating themselves up the same way they were beaten up.

MARLO THOMAS

"The needle slides into the boy's soft skin like a straw pushed into the center of a freshly baked cake. Liquid ebbs out of the syringe, replaced by bright red blood. The blood is then reinjected into the child." On September 28, 1980, these words, along with a shocking story about an eight-year-old heroin addict, appeared on the front page of the *Washington Post.* It was a lurid, incredible story. But it wasn't true.

The story's author, Janet Cooke, came to the *Post* with supposedly impeccable credentials: She had graduated with honors from Vassar and had won a writing award while at her hometown paper, the *Toledo Blade.* When she was hired by the prestigious *Post,* Cooke was assigned to the Weeklies section, where reporters hone their craft on lighter neighborhood stories before moving on to the national news sections. Cooke felt stuck there and was looking for a way to break out. The story "Jimmy's World" was it.

When Cooke won the Pulitzer prize for the story, editors at the *Blade,* proud of their alumna, began preparing a story and noticed major inconsistencies in her résumé. When word was passed along to her colleagues at the *Post,* they confronted Cooke. She first admitted only to the phony résumé, but after hours of needling and questioning, she broke down and told them that "Jimmy's World" was fictitious. She offered her resignation, and the *Post* ran an editorial apologizing to its readers and gave back the prize.

Why did Cooke do it? According to those who know her, her desire to break out of the Weeklies section was only a small part of the story. At the root of her troubles was a controlling father. As a young girl in Toledo, Cooke learned to lie as a defense against her demanding dad. To appease his imperious style of fathering, she played with the truth, and it soon became second nature to her. "Lying, from a very early age," said Cooke in the aftermath of the *Post* ordeal, "was the best survival mechanism available. And I became very good at it."

Lying is just one of countless destructive qualities that controlling parents unwittingly cultivate in their children. Others include being intimidated or hypersensitive to criticism. When these children become adults, they may also be afraid of becoming intimate with others or of becoming too dependent on someone else. They are often overly judgmental of people around them. The point is, growing up with a Pushy Parent has numerous negative repercussions, some of which have been felt over the centuries. Literally.

> You love me so much, you want to put me in your pocket. And I should die there smothered.
>
> D. H. LAWRENCE

Two hundred years ago experts urged parents to control their children "from the very beginning by means of scolding and the rod."[1] Parents were warned that willfulness and wickedness appear in the first year of life when children "see something they want but cannot have; . . . become angry, cry, and flail about." What is a parent to do? "The moment these flaws appear in a child, it is high time to resist this evil so that it does not become ingrained through habit." In the second and third years of life, parents were advised to devote themselves to instilling "a strict obedience" in their children. This is tough to do, warned the experts, because "it is quite natural for the child's soul to want to have a will of its own." Successful parents, however, will eventually benefit: "If [the children's] wills can be broken at this time, they will never remember afterwards that they had a will."

Though force and the the rod are no longer recommended by child-raising experts, squelching a child's spirit through over-controlling behavior is still in practice—even with adult children. It is seen when parents are overprotective, dictatorial, overly strict, belittling, manipulative, smothering, harsh, reserved, tense, irritable, stifling, unemotional, or pushy.

DO YOU HAVE A PUSHY PARENT?

The following self-test can help you assess whether you are in a relationship with a Pushy Parent. Circle *Y* if the statement is true of you or one of your parents. Circle *N* if the statement does not apply to this person.

Y   N   **1.** Do you feel as if you are living your life to please others?

Y   N   **2.** Was your home life designed primarily to please your parents, rather than to foster optimal growth for you and your siblings?

Y   N   **3.** Would most people agree that this parent is over-the-top on control issues?

Y   N   **4.** When you were growing up, did you feel pressured by excessive expectations or unattainable standards?

Y   N   **5.** When you were growing up, were you afraid to express anger, fear, or sadness around one of your parents?

Y   N   **6.** In retrospect, did either or both of your parents often violate your privacy or belittle you?

Y   N   **7.** As an adult, have you often felt intimidated or easily angered around controlling people?

Y   N   **8.** As an adult, do you often feel that it has taken a long time to emotionally separate from one or both of your parents?

Y   N   **9.** To this day, do you often feel you cannot fully please your parents?

Y   N   **10.** As an adult, do you feel tense when you think about a parent coming to visit?

Scoring: Total the number of Ys you circled. If you circled five or more Ys, you are certainly in a relationship with a Pushy Parent.

WHY PARENTS PUSH

Your parents' overcontrolling behavior is probably fueled by two misbeliefs: "My child *owes* me," and "I *own* my child."

All parents want to be appreciated and loved by their children. Healthier parents recognize that appreciation is a gift their children *may* give, not something they *must* give. Controlling parents, however, don't see it that way. They feel entitled to their children's love. That's why they demand that their children love, appreciate, listen to, and admire them. After all, their children *owe* them that. And because controlling parents believe that they *own* their children, they feel justified in their controlling ways.

Beneath these misbeliefs, however, is a myriad of reasons your mom or dad may have been overcontrolling. Resentment, for example, can be a motivator. If your parents believe you didn't have to "suffer" as they did as children, they may turn their resentment into overcontrol. Jay Ward, the creator of the famous Rocky and Bullwinkle cartoons, was so exasperated with the elaborate plans being made for his daughter's wedding ceremony, he simply didn't attend—a common tactic for Control Freaks who don't get their own way. Instead, he placed a tuxedo-clad dummy of himself at the entrance to the reception hall. Inside was a tape-recorded loop of Ward's voice greeting guests with the words, "Hello, my name is Jay Ward. This is costing me a fortune. Hello, my name is Jay Ward. This is costing me a fortune," over and over. Resentment can cause some parents to do some crazy things.

Another major force behind some controlling parental behavior is the surge of assurance it brings.[2] Some mothers, for example, find in their mothering role the power that has eluded them all of their lives. They find that their self-esteem is buoyed by their role as the person in charge, the person who knows what to do and how to do it. Such a mother, dependent and weak in all of her other relationships, thrives in her omnipotent-caretaker role, a role that depends, however, on her children remaining powerless and inadequate.

> Fathers and mothers have lost the idea that the highest aspiration they might have for their children is for them to be wise . . . specialized competence and success are all that they can imagine.
>
> ALLAN BLOOM

A simple lack of social savvy can also add to a Pushy Parent's persona. Brilliant musician and composer Gustav Mahler is a good example. A woman I was counseling some time ago asked me to read Mahler's autobiography because she felt his behavior was so much like that of her controlling father. She had flagged a page where it recounts the day a young composer came to the maestro's studio, hoping to gain Mahler's endorsement of a newly written opera. Mahler, like my client's controlling parent, had no concept of how to protect the young man from total disappointment. When the young composer had finished playing a part of the opera, Mahler did not utter a word. The young composer put on his coat, wrapped up the score, and sheepishly left the room. All of Mahler's experiences and personal relationships had not supplied him with an ounce of social polish that could have brought the meeting to a satisfactory end.[3] It is this kind of social ineptness, coupled with a drive for perfection, that causes some parents to unwittingly plant land mines in the psyche of their kids. In fact, it was exactly what drove my client into a downward spiral that eventually caused her to consider taking her own life. The power of a Pushy Parent is almost unimaginable.

Perhaps the most important cause of controlling behavior in some parents is the trauma they suffered early in their own lives.[4] They may have experienced stunning pain or loss as children. And psychologically, we know that if people experience an unexpected or shocking event that isn't resolved—they lose a parent or even a pet and are simply told to "keep a stiff upper lip"—they may spend decades trying to get over it. One method for doing so is to become over-protective and strict with one's own children. *Since I couldn't control my own childhood,* the reasoning goes, I'm going to control my child.

> It is when power is wedded to chronic fear that it becomes formidable.
>
> ERIC HOFFER

Whatever the reasons behind your parent's overcontrolling behavior, one thing is for sure: You don't have to be controlled by him or her any longer. You can cope. In fact, with time, you can find freedom from the tyranny of a parent who has tried to own you.

COPING WITH A PUSHY PARENT

Perhaps you're a college student still living at home and doing your best to cope with a father who wants to prescribe your daily schedule. Maybe you're thirtysomething and enjoy a successful career, but you find yourself reverting to feeling as if you are thirteen whenever your mother calls to find out why you haven't called her. Or perhaps your parents died years ago, but you're still hearing the tapes of their voices reminding you that you never measured up or that your desires don't really matter. Whatever your state, if you have or have had controlling parents, here are some of the most effective ways for moving out from under their thumbs.

Put Yourself in Your Pushy Parent's Shoes

This may be the toughest part of this chapter for some people, but it is an exercise that will pay tremendous dividends if you do it. I'm asking you to imagine yourself in your controlling parent's position. What was life like for your controlling parent? Where did your dad or mom grow up, and what were the conditions in his or her childhood home? What was your Pushy Parent's relationship like with his or her parents? What kind of parental models did your grandparents provide? What was your mom or dad like as a child? Did he or she suffer any traumatic events you are aware of? And what was it like for your Pushy Parent in the workplace? Was he or she in a powerful position that may have contributed to controlling tendencies at home? Or was your dad or mom in a position that got little respect from others? Did that lead to your getting pushed around at home?

I don't know what your mom's or dad's life has been like, but I can tell you that the more you try to understand it and see it as he or she does, the more likely you are to cope more effectively with your present problem. If you want to take this a step further, you may even want to delve into your parent's past by interviewing your mother or father. You can also interview your controlling parent's relatives and friends. This can be very fruitful if it is done with the goal of simply wanting to understand what life was like for him or her.

> We all agree that forgiveness is a beautiful idea until we have to practice it.
>
> C. S. Lewis

Empathy, that practice of seeing the world through someone else's eyes, helps us bring more grace and more love into our character. Empathy, more than any other human quality, helps us cultivate patience with another person. It helps us ease up and relax a bit more. So, I urge you right from the beginning, before you go on to the next few steps, to pause for a moment and imagine what life would have been like if you had lived it in your Pushy Parent's shoes.

Get a Reality Check

The first step in making peace with your controlling parent is to understand just how controlling he or she was or is. Child development experts generally agree that too little parental control is as bad as too much. Only the most inept parents do not set limits or restraints with their kids. The question, of course, is how much control is too much? When does a parent's authority become too heavy-handed? To help you find the answer for your specific situation, you may want to talk to friends you trust or even consult a counselor. The goal is to determine whether you're making too much out of the typical control most parents wield or whether you are dealing with a certifiable Control Freak parent.

Find the Good in Your Parent's Control

Just this week I took my annual trek to the card store to get a card for my mom. I fumbled through dozens of impersonal Mother's Day cards to find the one I thought she would appreciate most. After reading a few poetic and flowery greetings and well wishes, I quickly turned my attention to the humorous cards. One in particular caught my attention. It pictured a mother driving a car with her outstretched arm protectively flung across her son's chest as he innocently sits in the passenger seat. The message said it all: "To Mom, the original seat belt."

Truth is, we owe a lot to the protective instincts of both our moms and dads. Of course, since you are reading this chapter, you're probably not too concerned about the good that can be found in your parent's protective control. But that's the point of this step. Like the first two, this one will also help you build up your tolerance for overcontrolling parental tendencies. What I'm asking you to do is note the good things your Pushy Parent did for you. Though he or she was overcontrolling, what good things came out of that behavior anyway? Perhaps it was safety, as the card said. Or maybe it was a sense of deep care. Did his or her controlling ways help you cultivate a healthy sense of discipline in your life? Maybe none of these things occurred for you. But surely something good can be found in the relationship you have or had with your overcontrolling parent. Do your best to make a list, no matter how short, of ways your mom or dad made you a better person. This will engender an attitude of gratitude that has probably been running pretty low for you when it comes to your Pushy Parent. And this gratitude will benefit you with each step that follows.

> The greater the power, the more dangerous the abuse.
>
> EDMUND BURKE

Understand Your Parent's Pain

This step is similar to the first step I mentioned, but it takes it deeper. Once you have put yourself in your Pushy Parent's shoes, gotten a "reality check," and tried to look for the good in spite of the bad, you are ready to take a good, hard look at your parent's pain.

How much do you really know about your parent's roots? Did he or she experience trauma as a child? The reason I ask is that, more often than not, a controlling parent suffered some type of trauma as a child or young adult. Your parent may have grown up during a world war, the depression, or the Holocaust. Perhaps your mom or dad suffered the loss of a parent or faced a grave illness or life-threatening physical injury. Or maybe your Pushy Parent was physically abused by an alcoholic relative. Whatever the circumstances, there is a pretty good chance that a parent who is overcontrolling has suffered a traumatic life event. And chances are that if you take the time to understand it, you will have more sympathy and grace for your parent. This does not mean that your parent is not responsible for the way that he or she has treated (or is treating) you. Asking your controlling parent about his or her childhood is for your benefit. It will help you more effectively cope with the control issues.

Set Healthy Boundaries

In a counseling session, a woman once confided in me: "My mother used to tell me, 'I know you better than you know yourself.' She figured that made it okay to run my life." My client went on to tell me that it took her several years as an adult to recognize that her mother didn't know her that well and that she could make decisions for herself—even when they were not in line with her mother's wishes. In other words, she was drawing a line and setting boundaries. You can do the same thing. You, more than anyone else, know what you want, need, think, and feel. Sure, you can ask for input from others when you want to, but you do not have to make every decision to meet an overcontrolling parent's approval—not if you set boundaries.[5]

Just last week I was speaking at a conference in Tucson, Arizona, and at the close of the afternoon session, I met with a fellow speaker, psychologist Henry Cloud, for dinner. He and John Townsend probably have done more to help people establish healthy boundaries in relationships than any other people I know. They coauthored a best-selling book, appropriately titled *Boundaries: When to Say Yes and When to Say No to Take Control of Your Life.* One of the many things I have learned from these two experts is that if you don't set boundaries with pushy people, you are diminishing the ability for you and that person to lead a healthy life. Saying no, in other words, is not a selfish act on your part. It may be one of the most caring things you can do. I urge you to put this principle into practice. Start small if you want. Choose something little, like what time your Pushy Parent is wanting to pick you up for a meeting. You have a right to establish your own agenda. Success in setting

> The more we idealize the past and refuse to acknowledge our childhood sufferings, the more we pass them on unconsciously to the next generation.
>
> ALICE MILLER

boundaries with something relatively small will empower you to set boundaries on things that matter more—like what you name your child or whether you have children at all.

I talked with Claire, a woman whose controlling mother was pushing her to have children. It got to the point that the mother was talking about it in public, at dinner parties, and so on, to embarrass her daughter, hoping that the embarrassment would motivate Claire to have a family. Eventually Claire had enough and found the courage to set a boundary. "Mother, I know you want another grandchild, but that is a decision between Todd and me. I don't like it that when we are in public together, you think that you can goad me into getting pregnant by criticizing me. I need you to stop doing that. Will you please not talk about it the way you've been doing?" Claire went on to give her mother specific examples of what she had been doing, and she made it clear that she would no longer put up with it. Claire promised her mother that if she ever publicly criticized Claire's unwillingness to have a child, Claire would refuse to go places with her mother. Thankfully, Claire never had to do that. The simple act of setting the boundary was enough to get her controlling parent under control.

Dare to Make a Meaningful Connection

In playwright Moss Hart's autobiography, he recalls a childhood Christmas when his father took him shopping. The two walked the New York streets, inspecting merchandise displays. Hart's eyes were drawn to a toy printing press. His father, a poor man, had less expensive things in mind, but he was reluctant to say so. "I heard my father jingle some coins in his pocket," Hart writes. "In a flash I knew it all. He'd gotten together about seventy-five cents to buy me a Christmas present, and he hadn't dared say so in case there was nothing to be had for so small a sum." Hart describes the despair and disappointment in his father's eyes and

> Parents tend to underestimate the enormous power their loving approval wields over the young child.
>
> ERNA FURMAN

how that brought him closer to his father. He then writes: "I wanted to throw my arms around him and say, 'It doesn't matter. . . . I understand. . . . I love you.' But instead we stood shivering beside one another for a moment and started silently back home. . . . I didn't even take his hand on the way home, nor did he take mine."[6]

Have you ever felt that way with your mom or dad? We so often find it awkward to make a meaningful connection and say what we really feel. But when we do, we not only feel better ourselves, but we are also opening up the channels for a healthier connection with our parents. We are melting the cold, dominant ways of the sometimes overcontrolling parent. Take the risk to make a meaningful connection. Reach out—even when part of you is feeling hesitant.

Forgive As Best You Can

Forgiveness does not mean forgetting or excusing. It means facing a wrongdoing, experiencing the feelings connected with being wronged, and, after a period of time that only you can determine, letting go of actively holding the wrongdoing against the wrongdoer.[7] The result is a restoration of your general sense of trust and love.

Ever since I was a child, I have enjoyed the biblical story of Joseph. It is a touching example of how a bad thing can turn good when forgiveness enters the picture. Joseph's older brothers were jealous of the attention their father gave to their younger brother, and they sold him into slavery, telling their father that he had been killed. Through twists and turns, Joseph ended up in Egypt, where he became a leader and was elevated to a place second only to the pharaoh. Years later, when famine came, Joseph's brothers traveled to Egypt to buy food and were brought before the prime minister, who, of course, was Joseph himself. When they recognized him, they were reminded of their selfish, evil deed to sell him to slave traders. They begged Joseph to forgive them. Rather than refuse to give them food or banish them, Joseph answered:

"As far as I am concerned, God turned into good what you meant for evil" (Gen. 50:20). Joseph forgave his brothers in order to restore the relationship. That's what forgiveness does.

Since childhood, I've been amazed that someone could forgive other people who treated him so badly—especially when they were his own family members. Joseph is an inspiration. His story continues to show me how courageous forgiveness is. And as I mature, I've learned that when we forgive, the very act of forgiveness provides us with more courage to look past our woundedness. It's almost inhuman. Divine. As my former seminary professor and friend Lew Smedes said, "When we forgive, we walk in stride with the forgiving God."[8]

> Animals kill their young if they don't want to care for them, but they don't torture them for years.
>
> ALICE MILLER

One more thing about forgiveness. It is essential to recognize that forgiveness has its own timing. It can be nurtured but never pushed. Premature forgiveness is guaranteed to backfire. "Let bygones be bygones," your friends may urge. Their comments, however well intentioned, often reflect their own discomfort rather than your needs. You were pressured enough growing up; don't pressure yourself into forgiving before you are ready.

Identify Your Reactive Style

One of the most important things you can do to step out of the rut most controlled children find themselves in is to explore your earliest coping strategy. As a child, did you comply with your controlling parent by doing whatever he or she wanted? Or did you rebel against your parent's wishes? Maybe you distracted yourself and your parent from this behavior by clowning around. Some children simply escape the control by giving up their spirit and numbing themselves to parental demands. Did you do this? Or did you try to gain parental favor by being more perfect than your parent could have hoped for? If you take the time to carefully examine your reaction to your parent's overcontrol, you will discover that it is probably still influencing your relationship with the parent today.

The bottom line is that this exercise in self-examination will help you to change unhealthy patterns in your life so that you are no longer compulsively driven to overachieve or automatically tempted to rebel or involuntarily compelled to turn inward and shut out stress, and so on.

A school of thought in psychology says that "awareness is often curative." I tend to agree. Once you become aware of something you are doing, you then make a choice as to whether you will keep doing it, or you will choose to change your behavior. The point is that you can't make the choice until you know it's yours. Take this step of self-examination seriously, and discover what you may need to do in the aftermath of coping with a controlling parent.

Meet Your Internalized Parent

If your thoughts and feelings were devalued by a controlling parent, you've probably inherited an endless recording that goes round and round like a loop in your mind: "I'm not as good as other people," or "No one really respects me." Whatever your internalized parental message says, chances are it's causing you to underrate your abilities, undercut your potential, or underplay your strengths. And this, in turn, is causing you to banish parts of your personality, present a false front to others, or see yourself as an object instead of a person. But remember, you don't have to give in to these messages. You can recognize them for what they are—distortions. You can heal them.

> Don't make your children angry by the way you treat them. Rather, bring them up with the discipline and instruction approved by the Lord.
>
> EPHESIANS 6:4

Just how does one go about finding healing from the years of self-devaluing messages from a parent? There are no "three easy steps" for this one. It often takes months, even years, for some who've been especially hurt or abused to find true inner peace and move beyond the pain. If you carry deep wounds from a Pushy Parent, I urge you to seek professional help from a minister or counselor who is trained in helping people work through such issues.

Make a Choice—and Know What It Is

Everyone with a controlling parent eventually makes a decision. Some people choose to learn that safety resides in other people's control, so they end up rarely making decisions for themselves. Other people feel compelled to spend all their time undoing their former powerlessness by acquiring the accoutrements of power—wealth or fame or prestige. Still others conclude that if they ever again allow anyone to get too close, he or she is going to control them, so they stay clear of genuine relationships. And some people simply learn that control is their parent's way of caring. They simply give him or her the benefit of the doubt to make peace with their past and the present.

The question is what choice are you going to make? Not making a choice, of course, is a choice in itself. Everyone with a controlling parent makes a decision. Everyone shapes his or her own interpretation of why Mom and Dad did what they did. And that interpretation just may be the most powerful way of coping with a controlling parent. Like painters choosing how to interpret their subject, you will eventually interpret your parent's controlling behavior. And when you do, will you place your parent in a positive frame or a negative frame? The choice is yours. Nobody else can make this choice for you. I'm simply suggesting that you make your choice, whatever it is, consciously. It is this choice and this clarity that will eventually help you reach closure on being raised by a Control Freak.

Break the Chain of Overcontrol

Is there a pattern of parental control in your family heritage, a pattern that has been handed down for generations? Maybe it is something that began in your family of origin. Either way, if you are a parent, you don't have to use the same dictatorial tactics. You can avoid passing them on to your own children.

There is no job that is harder or more important than parenting. It is immensely demanding—physically, emotionally, financially, and mentally. There are no perfect parents. All parents make mistakes. And research has shown us that we are far more likely to pass down the same mistakes our parents made if we do not consciously reverse the trend. So pay special attention to how you use control with your children. Beware of your own over-controlling tendencies as well as an excessively permissive parenting style that is developed in reaction to your parents' high standards.

When it comes to parents, nearly everyone can find something to complain about. Your parents probably complained about their parents, and your kids will probably complain about you. It seems to be an inevitable part of the parent-child relationship. And it may be justified. If your childhood felt like a scene from *Mommie Dearest* or *The Great Santini,* you have every right to complain about having a controlling parent. But once you've grown tired of complaining, it's time to move one, give up your grumbling, make peace with your past, and begin living without allowing your upbringing to bring you down.

10

THE INVASIVE IN-LAW

Tell her that if she's not in the church at four on the nose, we'll start the wedding without her.

GROOM'S FATHER OVERHEARD BEFORE THE WEDDING

Someone once observed that Adam and Eve got along as well as they did because neither had any in-laws to worry about. Maybe so. One can only imagine how having in-laws might have compounded their problems.

It seems some blessed couples couldn't be happier with their in-laws, while other couples feel their in-laws are the source of most of their problems. If you tend to identify more with the latter group, you are not alone. Experts believe that three-quarters of all married couples have problems with their in-laws. And the number one in-law problem is, without a doubt, controlling and intrusive behavior.[1]

Some in-laws smother and hover over a marriage without making room for the couple to have privacy, dabbling in things that aren't their business. Winston Churchill's "darling Clementine" learned early that she had married not just her husband but his strong-willed mother as well. When Winston and his wife returned from their honeymoon, the young bride discovered that Lady Randolph Churchill had completely redecorated the couple's new home in a style far fancier than Clementine had planned.

If you don't identify with Clementine or anyone else having in-law problems, count yourself blessed and in the minority. Most couples struggle to some degree with their partner's parents. This chapter is devoted to keeping your in-laws from becoming out-laws.

DO YOU KNOW AN INVASIVE IN-LAW?

The following self-test can help you assess whether you are in a relationship with an Invasive In-Law. Circle *Y* if the statement is true of one of your in-laws. Circle *N* if the statement does not apply to this person.

Y   N   **1.** I've never really felt as if this person has given us a blessing in our marriage.

Y   N   **2.** I often feel judged or critiqued by this person.

Y   N   **3.** This person seems to want to know everything that is going on between my spouse and me.

Y   N   **4.** This person wants to have a say in things that are none of his or her business.

Y   N   **5.** Other people I know would say that this person can be an overcontrolling person.

Y   N   **6.** I sometimes feel that this person is snooping into the private side of my marriage.

Y   N   **7.** It sometimes feels that whatever I do, I can't seem to set boundaries that stick with this person.

Y   N   **8.** This person just can't seem to keep quiet when it comes to giving me advice.

Y   N   **9.** At times I have been tempted to move farther

away from this person or not take his or her
phone calls.

Y   N   **10.** Given the opportunity, this person would control
everything from how my home is decorated, to
where we go on vacations, to how we should
raise our children.

Scoring: Total the number of Ys you circled. If you circled five
or more Ys, you are certainly in a relationship with an Invasive
In-Law.

WHY IN-LAWS INVADE

Twenty-eight-year-old Jamie was married just over a year when she
discovered her mother-in-law, Rita, was a major-league intrusive
in-law. It was on a day when Jamie's husband was off at work and
Jamie was sick in bed that Rita dropped by with some hot soup.
Rita let herself into the house and quietly tiptoed up to Jamie's
bedroom to find her daughter-in-law fast asleep. That's when Rita
decided to go the kitchen and prepare lunch. Sometime later
Jamie awoke and wandered bleary eyed downstairs to find Rita
sitting in their living room reading a book.

"Well, there you are, sleepyhead," Rita said to a startled
Jamie. "I thought you might sleep all day. It's probably the best
thing for you. Are you feeling better? I've got some of Jack's favorite soup waiting for you in the kitchen."

"What! Did Jack let you in?"

"I hope you like tomato bisque, honey."

Jamie had some of the soup Rita prepared for her, took some
medication, and then went back to her bedroom for more rest.
Later that evening when Jamie's husband was home and Jamie
was feeling a little better, she came into the kitchen for a glass of
juice. When she opened the cupboard where her drinking glasses
were stored, they were gone. Instead, it was filled with dishes.

Jamie quickly looked through the other cupboards and then the drawers. Every one of them had been reorganized with totally different items. Silverware that had once been in a drawer near the dishwasher was now down by the refrigerator, and so on.

"Jack, did you rearrange the kitchen?" Jamie asked her husband.

Turns out that Rita, without asking a soul, completely redid Jamie's kitchen while Jamie was asleep upstairs. "I can't believe her, Jack. Why? Why does she do this kind of thing?"

Jamie, like every other victim of in-law intrusiveness, was at her wit's end. She was completely befuddled and desperate to explain her insensitive mother-in-law's behavior.

Well, I don't know the specifics of Rita's situation, but after working with numerous situations just like this, I can give you some of the most common reasons why some in-laws don't know the meaning of personal boundaries.

> A wise parent humors the desire for independent action so as to become the friend and advisor when his absolute rule shall cease.
>
> ELIZABETH GASKELL

To begin with, it's important to realize that some in-laws are major-league Control Freaks across the board. That is, they are not singling out you or anyone else. Dominating is simply their general mode of operation. So, welcome to the family of a Control Freak. Try not to take it personally.

Other in-laws seem to make interfering in your life a quality they seemingly reserve just for you. While they are fairly easygoing with most other people, they can't help but give you advice and probe into your personal affairs. Why? Probably because you are seen as a potential threat. Now, you probably have never intentionally done anything to make your intrusive in-law feel uncomfortable. But that's beside the point. It's not what you have done or even who you are that matters. It's the place you have taken. Just as a firstborn child often feels threatened or even dethroned by a younger sibling, your in-laws may feel that you have taken (or will take) their place in their son's or daughter's life. And in a sense you have (or will).

The point is that when some folks feel endangered, they behave in strange and even nasty ways. As the saying goes, a threatened kitten becomes a tiger. And in a similar vein, threatened parents become Control Freaks. Where they were once kind and easygoing, they criticize and try to dominate. If this sounds familiar, your main concern is probably not why they do what they do, but what you can do about it.

> Love is proved in the letting go.
>
> C. Day Lewis

COPING WITH INVASIVE IN-LAWS

Most people discover their Invasive In-Laws before they get married. The news may even sink in before a couple becomes engaged. While you are dating, your partner's parents may give you the third degree, for example. They interrogate you to see if you are fit to date their son or daughter. They may give explicit dictates about dating. If you do not see the control during the dating period, however, the issues usually reveal themselves during the wedding preparations. I once heard a new father-in-law say to some of his friends at the wedding reception, "If I had let them do the wedding, the whole thing would have been a disaster. It's not as if they're paying for it." Wherever and whenever you discovered that you had an in-law who likes to take control of your life, the following advice will help you regain it.

Put Yourself in Your Invasive In-Laws' Shoes

If you have read any of the other chapters in part 2 of this book, you could probably predict that I would begin my suggestions for coping with Invasive In-Laws with this first step: Empathy. It is at the heart of making any bad relationship better. Once again, I suggest you do your best to see the world through the eyes of your in-laws.

> Oh, what a tangled web do parents weave when they think that their children are naive.
>
> Ogden Nash

Empathy requires both your heart and your head. That's what makes it so rare. You need to use your heart to feel what your in-laws are feeling. And you need to use your head to analyze whether this feeling you perceive is, in fact, accurate. If you will take the time to do this—to imagine what the world looks and feels like to your Invasive In-Laws—you will have primed the pump to put the following principles into practice.

You may be wondering how you can more completely empathize with your in-laws. It happens when you try to get to know them better. It happens when you ask more questions, not just about what's going on now, but about what life was like when they were growing up. It occurs when you ask questions about their own marriage and work. The more you get to know your in-laws, the more understanding you will have of their circumstances and makeup. Take the plunge, even right now, and imagine for a moment what your life would be like if you were the in-law and your son or daughter married you.

Face the Problem Head-On

One of the worst mistakes any couple can make in dealing with difficult in-laws is to pretend the problem doesn't exist. Some hold out the hope that the situation, without any effort of their own, will magically get better. So, one of my first recommendations in building a better relationship with your in-laws is to face the problem head-on.

Todd and Julie realized they had a major Invasive In-Law problem with Todd's dad. Shortly after they were married, Todd's dad began calling their apartment "just to check in." He would ask them about everything from how they were decorating their living room to whether they had enough canned tuna stocked up in the kitchen cabinets. It didn't matter whether it was Todd or Julie who answered the phone when he called, he would rattle off a string of questions about things that were none of his business. This went on sporadically through their first two years of marriage. Todd and Julie thought it was kind of cute at first, but

> For the sake of one good action, a hundred evil ones should be forgotten.
>
> CHINESE PROVERB

soon it became tiresome. They wondered what to do. *Maybe he'll get tired of it sooner or later,* they thought. *Or maybe if we cut the calls short by excusing ourselves for something, he will get the message; we don't want to hurt his feelings.* After more than two years, when they finally decided enough was enough, they faced the problem head-on.

"Mom and Dad, Julie and I want to talk to you about something," Todd said to his father as the four of them sat in a booth around a table at a restaurant. "We really appreciate how helpful you've been to us as we've been getting started in our marriage, but sometimes we feel as if we need to have a bit more space."

"What are you saying?" Todd's father quickly asked.

"Well, Dad, maybe if you'd let us call you sometimes instead of your calling us so often."

"Yes," Julie chimed in. "We love knowing that you are interested in what's going on for us, but some evenings we spend more time talking to you on the phone than we do talking to each other."

Todd's mom began to help out. "Honey, you do call them an awful lot, and they deserve to have more space."

"You're right," the father quickly assented. He then proceeded to tell them how he felt so isolated from his own parents when he first got married and that he didn't want the same thing to happen to them. "I can see now that I've overreacted, and I'll pull back."

> As we grow in wisdom, we pardon more freely.
>
> ANNE-LOUISE-GERMAINE DE STAËL

The confrontation need not be hurtful. In fact, it is always best to do it in a way that honors your in-law. Todd and Julie did this by making it clear how much they appreciated Todd's dad. He did not feel attacked; if anything, he felt relieved to know that his kids were not feeling neglected.

You may take comfort in knowing that most married couples struggle with in-law problems to some degree, but don't allow that fact to make you complacent. If you try to ignore the problem, it will only get bigger. The time to make the situation better is now.

Work as a Team

Once you admit to yourself that a problem exists, you need to share your concerns with your spouse. This can be a tricky task. Take special care to avoid putting your partner on the defensive. He or she may see it as a personal attack if you blurt out your frustration. You may want to begin by asking questions: "Do you ever feel as if your parents meddle in our marriage?" This will open the door to a more civil discussion. You may be in agreement about the situation, but if you aren't, take the time to hear out your spouse. If he or she doesn't see it the way you do, remain calm, and when appropriate, share why you see things differently. This is critical to solving the problem. You must work as a team. If it is not already crystal clear to both sets of parents, make sure they know that your marriage is your priority.

Todd and Julie are a good example. Julie was the one who first noticed the problem with Todd's dad and eventually brought it up with Todd. It was news to him. He hadn't even noticed it until Julie pointed it out, and after an initial period of defending his father, he soon saw how his dad's calls were interfering with their time at home. That allowed them to approach the problem as a team. The confrontation never would have worked if Julie had been left to deal with the problem on her own. In fact, that would have guaranteed a major marital problem.

If your spouse is not quite as receptive as Todd was, be patient and give your partner concrete examples of his or her parent's invasiveness when it happens. This will help your spouse see things as you do. Once you are both seeing the situation from the same perspective—more or less—you are ready to establish a specific plan of action. But even if you don't come to complete agreement on what's going on with your in-laws, many of the following recommendations can still be put into practice.

Win Them Over If You Can

One of the reasons you may be experiencing problems with Invasive In-Laws is that they don't know you or trust you or accept you. If, for example, you feel like an outsider around your partner's family, ask yourself if there is something you're doing or saying that's holding them back. Then ask yourself what you can do to win them over. Would it help to have some one-on-one time with your spouse's mom or dad? Are you doing something that might be perceived as threatening (e.g., breaking an unspoken family rule)? Are your aspirations not what they had hoped for? If so, maybe it would help to talk openly and calmly with your in-laws. Of course, the trick is not to get defensive. Work at understanding them rather than being understood by them.

> It is cheaper to pardon than to resent. Forgiveness saves the expense of anger, the cost of hatred.
>
> HANNAH MORE

If your best efforts to win them over seem to come up empty, it may be time for your partner to intervene and find out what's bothering your in-laws. If you go this route, however, your spouse must make his or her loyalty to you known to them. This helps prevent an emotional triangle from being formed. And you certainly don't want that. If your spouse feels caught in the middle because he or she is trying to ride the fence, your marriage will weaken and your frustration will compound. Besides, presenting a united front shows your in-laws that the two of you are really in love and that their child makes you happy. They may then realize that if their child loves and trusts you, perhaps they should too.

Take Back Your In-Laws' "Right" to Meddle

One of the most common reasons some in-laws smother a marriage is because they feel as if they have a right to. Where would such an idea come from, you ask? Usually from a financial string that keeps them tightly tied to you. If you are feeling smothered, it may be because you have not yet unhooked yourself financially. Of course, the indebtedness may not be only financial. It could be that you are relying on Mom and Dad for regular child care because it is convenient and cheap. However, this kind of favor is not always as "cheap" as you might think. So, consider why your in-laws might feel that they have a right to meddle in your marriage, and then do something to change it.

Only you will know what that "something" is, and the best way to detect it is to ask what you are most indebted to your in-laws for. Did they give you some of their best furniture as a gift that has strings attached? Then cut the cords by replacing it if you can or giving it back if need be. Or maybe they've offered to pay your rent for the first year of your marriage. As hard as it might be to give this up, you may find doing that easier than paying the emotional price of having intrusions because of their gift. These are tough calls, especially for newlyweds who have limited resources. The point is that you should at least explore whether there is something in your circumstances that is giving your in-laws the "right" to meddle in your marriage. Then you'll at least know what you are dealing with.

> We all make many mistakes, but those who control their tongues can also control themselves in every other way.
>
> JAMES 3:2

Be in the "No" from Time to Time

Mindy's mother-in-law has been running a large and complicated family for decades. When Mindy married Don, she took her place in line with the other daughters-in-law, accepting family dinner and holiday assignments with the others. But she felt like a private in some domestic army. So, unlike one daughter-in-law, who refused to participate in any Christmas celebrations, Mindy decided to stand up to her mother-in-law in her own small way by setting a boundary. Mindy knew she couldn't respect herself if she followed family orders all the time. Therefore, every so often she gathered her courage and said a gentle polite no.

The issue is irrelevant. Over the years, her refusals have ranged from "No, I don't want to bake the ham" to "No, I don't think that's the best summer camp for the kids." The refusals don't come often, and they aren't aggressive or in-your-face, but they are frequent enough to remind her mother-in-law and everyone else that Mindy is a person operating under her own will.

Getting your way for the sake of registering your presence is a reasonable interpersonal technique. The trick is not to overdo it. The other daughter-in-law in this family created a catastrophe by asserting her personal power in a careless, dramatic, and extreme way. Rather than equalize her relationship with her mother-in-law, she destroyed it.

Mindy was neither pushy nor a pushover, and it got her the respect she knew she deserved.

Don't Allow In-Laws to Make Up Your Mind

Setting boundaries is an important consideration in dealing with your domineering in-laws. When they intrude, speak up. Let them know that you need some private time or space. Be polite but assertive. Don't feel obligated to offer explanations or apologize for your needs. Simply state your request, and stick to it. If, for example, they are expecting you to be at their home for Thanksgiving, never asking you for your input on the decision, you might say, "We have discussed it and decided together that this year we are going to celebrate Thanksgiving in our own home. You are welcome to join us if you like—we'd love to have you." This kind of decision lets your in-laws know that they cannot make up your mind for you, and it still allows them to be included in your life.

Make Plans Early for the Holidays

Few times are filled with more conflict between Invasive In-Laws and marriage partners than the holidays. Why? Because most couples, especially newlyweds, expect the holidays to be a perfect opportunity for bringing them closer together as they celebrate the season as husband and wife. Unfortunately the "happiest time of the year" often turns out to be one of the toughest on marriages. If choosing how to meld two families' holiday traditions were not enough for most couples, there is the quandary of whose home each holiday will be devoted to. If both families have strong Christmas traditions, for example, each one may expect you to spend the season with them. And since geography usually prevents you from splitting your time, there is bound to be disappointment and hurt feelings one way or the other. However, you can do something to make this situation easier on everyone involved: If both families are expecting you to join them for the holidays, make advanced announcements about what you plan to do. This gives everyone time to adjust their feelings before the big event.

> No matter how calmly you try to referee, parenting will eventually produce bizarre behavior, and I'm not talking about the kids. Their behavior is always normal.
>
> BILL COSBY

One creative solution I recently heard came from a couple who is part of a very large family where it was becoming next to impossible for all of the adult children and their spouses to get back to their parents' home on the same holiday. So they declared another day their "national family holiday." It became tradition for them to all gather on the first weekend in August. No matter what, they all made sacrifices and did whatever they had to do to be together from around the country on that weekend. That was their family "holiday," and it took the pressure out of Thanksgiving and Christmas in their homes. This creative idea may not work for everyone, but it worked great for them.

One more thing. Sometimes couples get caught in the trap of trying to please everyone but themselves. It is important that you focus on making your holiday special for the two of you and not just your families. For example, if your families live just hours apart, you might be considering splitting your time on Christmas Day between them. But think about spending most of that special day en route from one house to the other. Is that really what you want? If so, be sure you have adjusted your expectations accordingly.

When All Else Fails, Shift Gears

Once you have made every effort to build a better relationship
with your partner's parents, the issue has been put on the table
and opened for discussion, and your in-laws still
don't get the message, it is time to shift gears. At this
point, you need to begin thinking with your partner
about how to maintain your own sense of well-being
within this relationship. That may require setting
some pretty firm boundaries.

> Selective ignorance, a cornerstone of child rearing. You don't put kids under surveillance: it might frighten you. Parents should sit tall in the saddle and look upon their troops with a noble and benevolent and extremely nearsighted gaze.
>
> GARRISON KEILLOR

For example, you may need to set limits on how
often you and your partner get together with the in-
laws. While this may be difficult for your partner, he
or she needs to realize that bonding with you may
mean risking a more distant relationship with
parents. And more than likely, the parents will gain more respect
for you and your marriage. You might even see the relationship
with your in-laws improve as you work at maintaining your own
well-being.

The bottom line is that you can do only so much. After you
have done your best and given it time, it becomes your in-laws'
problem, not yours. However, if you are edging toward this position, don't neglect my final recommendation for coping with
Invasive In-Laws.

Take the Good with the Bad

As you set your boundaries with in-laws, take care not to throw
out the good with the bad. Sure, their nosy behavior gets under
your skin. Of course you don't appreciate their intrusions. But consider the good they bring to your relationship. Appreciate and respect them for who they
are. As you keep an eye out for the good, it will help
you swallow the bad more easily.

> The only way to have a friend is to be one.
>
> RALPH WALDO EMERSON

Along these same lines, accept that your in-laws, like any
other human beings, are imperfect. They aren't likely to change

radically at this point in their lives. So gain some tolerance for their nosy ways by learning more about them. In fact, it is a great diversion to ask them about their childhood, their courtship, their hobbies, and so on. Along the way you will probably gain some insights into their present behavior. Who knows, you might even end up *asking* them for their wisdom.

11

THE TENACIOUS TEEN

There are few situations in life that are more difficult to cope with than an adolescent son or daughter during the attempt to liberate themselves.

ANNA FREUD

Ask any sixteen-year-old for a definition of control, and you will hear something like "Getting to do what I want to do, when I want to do it." And ask that same teenager what keeps him or her from having control, and you'll hear something about his or her parents.

It's inevitable. Somewhere between childhood and adulthood, most of us journey through a time when Mom and Dad are seen as completely clueless. Mark Twain said it well: "When I was seven, my father knew everything. When I was fourteen, my father knew nothing. But when I was twenty-one, I was amazed how much the old man had learned in just seven years."

Adolescents, by definition, are struggling to affirm and assert their autonomy, which means they're no longer willing to define themselves as "daughter" or "son" or "child." Indeed, their passionate need to establish the right to a life of their own, their need to proclaim loudly, "I'm mine, not yours," is so urgent and so powerful that anything and everything becomes a battle for control.[1]

Think back to when you were sixteen, struggling to wrest control from the adults in your life—the ones who set rules and curfews. Your struggle to disengage from your parents' authority probably found you rebelling against most things too. You closed your ears to their sermons and rolled your eyes at their warnings.

As I said, conflict during this time is inevitable. Parents need to be needed. Adolescents tend not to need them. In his classic book *Between Parent and Teenager*, Haim Ginott said, "Teenagers are like a person needing a loan but wishing they were financially independent."[2] No wonder control is at stake for the Tenacious Teen.

The trouble comes, of course, in trying to give them the control they so desperately want. We can accept a preschooler who insists on certain kinds of routines. She may need a drink of water before going to bed, or she may want a particular doll with her in bed every night, and no other doll will do. She may insist that the same glass be used for her milk at every meal. It's all done in an attempt to give the child more control of her environment and her own behavior. The more predictable you can make her life, the more secure she feels.

But when that same child becomes an adolescent and begins to insist that she knows better than you when she should arrive home from a party or how much time she needs to study, we find ourselves in one of the most intense battles for control we will ever encounter. This chapter is dedicated to helping you find your way through this war zone.

DO YOU KNOW A TENACIOUS TEEN?

The following self-test can help you assess whether you are in a relationship with a Tenacious Teen. Circle *Y* if the statement is true of the teen you know. Circle the *N* if the statement does not apply to this person.

Y   N   **1.** If this teen knows I want him or her to do something, he or she will often do the opposite.

Y   N   **2.** This teen knows exactly how to push my buttons.

Y   N   **3.** This teen takes control by preventing me from knowing what's going on.

Y   N   **4.** I sometimes find myself going out of my way to avoid contact with him or her just to avoid having a conflict.

Y   N   **5.** This teen can be a perfect lady or gentleman around others but becomes a tyrant around me.

Y   N   **6.** This teen can literally exhaust me with pressure to get what he or she wants.

Y   N   **7.** I never quite know what kind of mood this teen will be in.

Y   N   **8.** If I'm honest, I sometimes feel myself regretting the way I treat this teen—but he or she continually drives me to do things I don't want to do.

Y   N   **9.** This teen sometimes blatantly lies to my face in order to get his or her own way.

Y   N   **10.** I feel as if I'm in a constant game of tug-of-war with this teen.

Scoring: Total the number of Ys you circled. If you circled five or more Ys, you are certainly in a relationship with a Tenacious Teen.

WHY TEENS ARE TENACIOUS

Teens, more than any other age group, feel out of control. Why? Because at their very core, deep down, they are not even sure who they are. Not yet. They are struggling to take possession of their very lives.

During World War II, pioneering developmental psychologist Erik H. Erikson coined a phrase that stuck—*identity crisis.* He used it to describe the disorientation of shell-shocked soldiers who could not remember their names. Over the years, this phrase has become a useful tool in describing the struggle of growing up.

Achieving a sense of identity is the major developmental task of the teenager—and it is the fuel in the tank of a Tenacious Teen.

Like stunned soldiers in a state of confusion, young people are hit sooner or later with a bomb that is more powerful than dynamite: puberty. Somewhere between childhood and maturity, their once reliable bodies kick into overdrive and change at an alarming rate. With this rapid acceleration of physical and emotional growth, they become strangers to themselves. Under attack by an arsenal of firing hormones, the bewildered young person begins to ask: *Who am I?*

> There are times when parenthood seems nothing but feeding the mouth that bites you.
>
> PETER DE VRIES

While achieving a meaningful answer to this question is a lifelong pursuit, it is the burning challenge of adolescence. According to Erikson, building an identity, knowing who you are, is what gives maturing adolescents an eventual sense of control. In the meantime, they are often grasping at anything that approximates the control they lack. You could say that this struggle for identity is gnawing the heart of every Tenacious Teen.

Without an identity, awkward adolescents carry a how-am-I-doing? attitude that is continually focused on the impression they are making on others. Without an identity, they will be or do whatever they think others want. They will flounder from one way of acting to another, never able to step outside of a preoccupation with their own performance and genuinely ask anyone, "How are you doing?" Erikson calls this miserable state "identity diffusion."[3]

The successful formation of an identity follows a typical pattern. Children identify with the people they admire. Young people emulate the characteristics of the people they want to be, whether they find these people in real life or through magazines and TV. By the end of adolescence, if all goes as it should, these identifications merge into a single identity that incorporates past identifications and also alters them to make a unique and coherent whole.

> If you bungle raising your children, nothing else matters much in life.
>
> JACQUELINE KENNEDY ONASSIS

The quest for identity is scary. Somewhere between ages twelve and twenty, adolescents are forced to choose who they are. It is a formidable task. Not sure which of their mixed emotions represent their true feelings, they are pushed to make up their mind. And once again they are compelled to control. Why? Because they did not choose this dismaying disequilibrium. It descended on them.

COPING WITH A TENACIOUS TEEN

Some years ago I wrote a book called *Helping the Struggling Adolescent*. It is a guide for parents and counselors who work with teens, and its focus is on solving the thirty most common problems kids encounter. I've received many letters from grateful readers who found the book helpful, but there was one person who wrote to pass on a principle to me. He gave me some tongue-in-cheek advice that came in the form of a chain letter. Here's what it said:

This chain letter is meant to bring relief and happiness to you. Unlike other chain letters, this one does not cost money. Simply send a copy of this letter to six other parents who are tired of their teenagers. Then bundle yours up and send him or her to the parent at the bottom of the list.

In one week, you will receive 16,436 teenagers, and you can keep one of them. Warning: One father broke the chain and got his own son back.

Have you ever felt that desperate in trying to cope with your Tenacious Teen? If so, you're not alone. But take heart, there's a better way. Experts have studied methods of taming Tenacious Teens for decades, and the following are some of the most effective methods known. They are, to say the least, more grounded than the help you would find from any chain letter. But beware, many of these strategies may go against the grain of a parent who is tired of his or her teenager. You will have to dig deep down in your character and call on God's strength to empower you with what you will need to succeed. This just may be the toughest job you ever had—beginning with the very first step.

Build a Platform of Kindness

Huston Smith, senior professor of religion at Syracuse University, wrote: "While I was teaching at MIT, Aldous Huxley joined us for a semester as distinguished visiting professor in the humanities. Needless to say, he was in demand all over New England, and my regard for him was so great that I volunteered to be his social secretary, driving him to and from his engagements because I wanted nothing so much that semester as to spend as much time in his presence as I could manage.

"On the way to one of his engagements, Huxley said, 'You know, Huston, it's rather embarrassing to have spent one's entire lifetime pondering the human condition and come toward its close and find that I really don't have anything more profound to pass on by way of advice than "Try to be a little kinder." ' "[4]

> In the life of children there are two very clear-cut phases, before and after puberty. Before puberty the child's personality has not yet formed, and it is easier to guide its life and make it acquire specific habits of order, discipline, and work; after puberty the personality develops impetuously and all extraneous intervention becomes odious, tyrannical, insufferable.
>
> ANTONIO GRAMSCI

If I were forced to sum up my advice on coping with a Tenacious Teen, I would have to come to the same sentence. Every struggling adolescent needs more kindness. No doubt about it. If you put yourself in his or her shoes and try to remember the pressure generated by having to build one's identity from scratch, you'll begin to recognize the value of trying to be a little kinder. Knowing just how to convey this kindness is the hard part. The following suggestions will help you do just that.

Own Your Part

Most parents feel joy and pride in their children's growing independence and accomplishments. However, parents may also find the loss of their roles, the takeover of their functions, hard to take. In her novel *Lovingkindness*, Anne Roiphe writes as a mother raising a girl into womanhood: "Our attractiveness dries as theirs blooms, our journey shortens just as theirs begins." She goes on to say, "Our replacements are eager for their turn, indifferent to our wishes, ready to leave us behind."[5] Consciously and unconsciously, parents may envy or resent the blossoming of youth in their teenagers. And it can cause them to tighten the screws and heighten their control just when they should be facilitating more independence. Take a good look in the mirror. Examine your own role in the tug-of-war, and own up to it if need be.

Look below the Surface

On a hike through the forests of the Olympic Peninsula in Washington State, I learned from a park ranger that when a tree is threatened, stressed by the elements of fire, drought, or other calamity, it twists beneath its bark to reinforce and make itself stronger. On the surface, this new inner strength may not be visible because the bark often continues to give the same vertical appearance. Only when the exterior is stripped away, or when the tree is felled, are its inner struggles revealed.

This is an important image to keep in mind whenever you're trying to cope with adolescents. They are masters at disguising their real feelings. Underneath the surface they may be struggling with unimaginable emotional pain or feelings of being pressured or stressed by parents or peers, but like a growing tree on the Olympic Peninsula, they twist and contort their secret emotions while giving off an appearance of feeling just fine. It takes a sensitive and patient person to look beyond the exterior emotions of an adolescent and realize that something else is going on inside.

Jake, a popular sixteen-year-old who did pretty well in the classroom but excelled on the football field, was driving his mother nuts. Literally. Jake had just gotten his driver's license and felt that it should also give him "license" to be treated like any other adult. He became more and more cocky. He no longer wanted to check in with his mom or ask permission for anything. And Jake was dead set on winning the all-out war of wills with his mom. Everything became a battle between the two of them. Whether it was what time he should get up in the morning for school or the parties he went to on the weekends or how he treated his younger brother—everything was a tug-of-war with Jake and his mom. "I don't understand," his mom confessed. "This kid has so much going for him. How can he complain?" And she was right. Jake was handsome, popular, a decent student, and a great athlete.

> Adolescence is a time of aching ambivalence, a time of both wanting to have—and surrender—control.
>
> JUDITH VIORST

What Jake's mom didn't know was that he suffered from extreme pressure. You see, three years earlier one of Jake's close friends, Tony, died when the car he was in was hit by a drunk driver. The afternoon before the accident, Jake and Tony had been tossing a football around in Jake's backyard, talking about their future as football players. And since the death, Jake had to wrestle not only with the usual grief that comes in losing a friend but also with a sense of responsibility to make his friend proud by making the starting string of the University of Washington football team. It was a secret he shared with no one except his grief counselor. The self-imposed pressure Jake was living under was almost crushing him.

Sure, Jake looks strong and sturdy on the outside, but inside he was twisting and contorting his emotional muscle just to stay standing. Only after earning his mother's trust did he eventually let her in on his silent pact with Tony. And when he did, his mother began to see Jake's tenacity in a whole new light.

Critique with Care

How can a parent of an adolescent give advice without his or her teenager perceiving it as showing disapproval, preaching sermons, imparting guilt, and, of course, meting out punishment? And how can a teenager not try to take control of his or her life by trying to avoid these things? "My dad gives me an hour lecture if I bring up something to him," says fourteen-year-old Jennifer. "I don't bother anymore." Talking to parents, many teens agree, runs the risk of making them upset. "There's no way I'd admit to my parents what I do on the weekend," says seventeen-year-old Kevin. They'd have a heart attack." So kids keep it inside. If they fear unwanted advice or disapproval, they talk it out with their friends. All this is to say that the more you are able to bite your tongue, the more likely it is that your Control Freak kid will open up to you. Critique with care. Here's what this might look like in a conversation that has potential to get nasty:

> The thing that impresses me most about America is the way parents obey their children.
>
> EDWARD, DUKE OF WINDSOR

Seventeen-year-old Kevin: I kind of scraped the passenger door on the Buick last night at my friend's house.

Dad: Yeah, Son, I noticed that this morning when I got the paper. Tell me what happened.

Kevin: Nothing. Some of us just got together. You know. Friday night.

Dad: Yeah, but how did the door get dented?

Kevin: I don't know. Jeff just kind of banged it with his car, I guess.

Dad: Were you in the car? Were you driving it at the time?

Kevin: I guess.

Dad: So it was all Jeff's fault?

Kevin: I don't know. Not really.

Dad: Well, what happened? It will just be easier if you put it out on the table and we deal with it.

Kevin: Dad, no matter what I say, I know you're going to go ballistic and tell me how immature I am, so why don't you just get it over with and start yelling at me?

Dad: Kevin, I know I've lost my temper with you in the past. I'm not going to do that, and I'm asking you to trust me. I just need to know what happened so we can take care of the insurance and so I know what you are doing with my car and whether you are in danger.

Kevin: Okay. Here goes. We were leaving this party and kind of joking about doing a drag race down the street because Jeff was driving his mom's minivan and I had your big Buick. We weren't going to really do it, but we were lining up like we were, and that's when the door got dented.

Dad (fighting every desire to holler): Okay *(long pause)*. Okay. I appreciate your honesty with me.

Kevin: I know it was stupid, Dad. I'll pay for whatever it costs.

By biting his tongue and refraining from trying to teach Kevin a driving lesson, Kevin's dad put the burden on his son's shoulders. Of course it's a risk, but if the dad had hauled off and scolded Kevin just to vent his own frustration, he never would have accomplished the same purpose. It never would have got Kevin to volunteer to talk. That's what critiquing with care is all about.

Look for the Good and Affirm It

Consider what might have happened if the great painter Benjamin West had not been affirmed by his mother. One day when he was a teenager, West's mother left him in charge of his little sister, Sally. While West's mother was gone, he discovered some bottles of colored ink and began to paint Sally's portrait. In doing so he made a huge mess of things. There were spilled bottles and ink blots everywhere.

When his mother came home, she saw the mess but said nothing. She picked up the piece of paper and saw the drawing. "Why," she said, "it's Sally!" and stooped and kissed her son. The little encouragement set Benjamin West on the path to be a professional painter. Even as an accomplished adult, West often said, "My mother's kiss made me a painter." Your Tenacious Teen may be waiting for that same kind of kiss from you. Sure, it's difficult to look past the mess and find the good, but it's worth the effort. It may even mark the turning point in your teenager's life.

> The most successful parents are those who have the skill to get behind the eyes of the child, seeing what he sees, thinking what he thinks, feeling what he feels.
>
> JAMES C. DOBSON

When your teen has friends over to your house and they make a mess of the kitchen, try to look past the extra work this creates for you and see the positive social value this brings to your son's or daughter's life. When your teen brings home a stray cat she found in the neighborhood, try to look past the impracticality of having an animal temporarily in your house and see the compassion and tenderness she has in trying to find the cat's owner. When your teen asks you to make pancakes at ten o'clock at night, try to look past your desire to go to bed and see it as a time to connect at the kitchen table. When your teen spends too much money on a jacket he bought at Nordstrom's, try to look past his dwindling budget and affirm his good fashion taste.

The point is to look for the good and affirm it—at least initially. Later, your teen's decision may need to be discussed and critiqued with care. But begin by looking for the good. It will ease your relationship and make your Tenacious Teen easier to live with.

Admit Mistakes and Be as Sincere as Possible

This may be a hard piece of advice to swallow, but if you want to disarm a controlling adolescent, you've got to admit when you are wrong and be sincere about your admission. The word *sincere* has an intriguing origin. It comes from two Latin words, *sine* and *cera*, which mean "without wax." In Roman days, some sculptors covered up their mistakes by filling the defects in their marble statues with wax, which was not readily visible until the statue had been exposed to hot sunlight. Dependable sculptors made certain that their customers knew the statues they sold were without wax by labeling them as *sine cera*. Of course, parents cannot simply hang out a sign that reads Sincere and expect others to see them as real. But we can be up-front about our mistakes by admitting when we have made them. Our tendency is to do just the opposite and cover our errors—to wax over them. But if you are vulnerable enough to admit your mistakes to a struggling adolescent, you may get the same vulnerability in return. Vulnerability begets vulnerability.

> It's frightening to think that you mark your children merely by being yourself. . . . It seems unfair. You can't assume the responsibility for everything you do—or don't do.
>
> SIMONE DE BEAUVOIR

When Rick realized that he had come down too hard on his daughter, Brenda, he decided to admit his overreaction. "Honey," Rick said to her, "you know I was very upset the other night when you came home nearly thirty minutes past the time we agreed on." Brenda sat silent, still fuming as her dad continued. "And to be honest, I didn't even listen to your reason for being late. I was so upset and frightened that I couldn't even hear what you were saying." Rick had his daughter's complete attention. "We care so much about you, and it just makes us scared. When I cut your curfew to punish you that night, I was probably overreacting in the heat of the moment. First of all, I want to apologize and say I'm sorry for not listening to you when you tried to tell me why you were late. I made a mistake. Can you accept my apology?" Brenda nodded yes and actually started to tear up. Her dad continued. "Second, I want to talk to you about what you think would be a fair way to respond to your being late so we don't find ourselves at this place again." The two of them went on to have a productive discussion about meeting curfews and how Brenda could keep her parents better informed—all because a parent admitted a mistake.

Beware of Rewards

Once there was an old man who was bothered by the noise of boys playing in his neighborhood. He offered to pay each kid a dollar to shout louder. The boys were delighted. But on the second day the man said his dwindling resources meant he could pay the boys only eighty cents. And on each succeeding day, he paid them less. Finally, the boys got angry and stopped playing near his house. "We're not gonna make noise for nothing!" they said.

Educational psychologists tell this story to illustrate an important principle: The best way to undermine kids' intrinsic interest in an activity is to reward them for doing it. And yet material rewards for schoolwork and everything else abound in homes in which parents are desperate to rein in their kids. Too many parents believe that rewards will encourage good behavior. But it's just not true. If your teenager already enjoys doing something that you appreciate, don't fall for the trap of rewarding it. The activity is reward enough for your youngster.

On the other hand, if you want your Tenacious Teen to do something he or she is not already doing, a reward can be quite useful. Say that you want your teenage son to help his younger sister with her math homework. Normally he tenaciously refuses to help. Rather than punishing him, try rewarding him with something he would enjoy on the weeks he helps her. Or say you want your daughter to answer your home telephone with a pleasant tone instead of her usually blunt "Who is it?" A small reward to reshape her behavior may do the trick. My point is that when it comes to controlling Tenacious Teens, you need to think through the behaviors you reward and the ones you don't.

> Build me a son, O Lord, who will be strong enough to know when he is weak and brave enough to face himself when he is afraid, one who will be proud and unbending in honest defeat, and humble and gentle in victory.
>
> DOUGLAS MACARTHUR

Don't Be Unrealistically Positive

Because adolescents' identities are shaped by how they believe others see them, they may change in order to contradict another person's perceptions, even if those perceptions are positive. In other words, it can be harmful to tell young people they won't have any problems, for example, that they are the best, or that they will someday be the greatest. Aware of their weaknesses, they will feel uncomfortable with an unrealistic positive appraisal that leaves no room for error. They will go out of their way to prove you wrong and relieve themselves from the burden of being perfect. For some, relief will come only in identifying with what they are least supposed to be, not in being something that is unattainable.[6]

Steer Clear of Regret

Elizabeth Forsythe Haily's best-selling novel *A Woman of Independent Means* tells the story of Bess Steed, an intrepid—and rather controlling—woman of the early twentieth century. Late in life she comes to realize that her attempts to control those she loved, especially her children, had backfired. She expresses this in a letter to her best friend: "I am determined not to repeat with my grandchildren the mistake I made with my children—using every means of coercion at my command, emotional as well as financial, to keep them close to me." She goes on to say that she has tried to take comfort in "duty visits" her children pay once a week, but in her heart she is bereft. "Polite strangers," she writes, "have taken the place of the two precious allies I sought to keep at my side forever." She concludes by saying, "No mother was ever more terrified of being abandoned in her old age than I—and no mother ever did more to make it happen by doing so much to prevent it."[7]

Learn the lesson Bess Steed learned, and don't try to

> In youth, everybody believes that the world began to exist only when he was born, and that everything really exists only for his sake.
>
> JOHANN WOLFGANG VON GOETHE

control your teenager so much that you end up driving him or her away forever.

Don't Make the Target Too Easy to Hit

I once knew a girl whose mother had tried hard to keep her daughter under strict sexual control the moment the girl hit puberty. "I don't want you doing this—you'll end up pregnant." "I don't want you going there—you'll end up pregnant." "I don't want you hanging around with him or her—you'll end up pregnant."

When the time finally came for this girl to rebel against her mother's control, she knew exactly where she wished to end up. You see, some parents of Tenacious Teens live in fear of their teenager doing the one thing that will embarrass them the most, so they harp on that one thing. And their doing so sends a distinct message to that young person: If you really want to hurt us, here is the best way to do it.

For some parents it may be attending church. They may let other things slide but never budge an inch when it comes to their child's being at every church service. Well, when that child is old enough and tenacious enough to want to strike back at the parents, he or she will do it by rebelling against the church. That is how the teen will regain control of the control he or she feels the parents have stolen.

For some parents it may be education. They may have hammered the message that to be successful and amount to anything in life, you have to go on for a college degree or maybe a Ph.D. The more the child is hit in the head with this message, the more he or she sees that by dropping out of high school, he or she can regain the control the parents have held on to.

I'm not saying that you should neglect the values and aspirations you have for your child. But if you are coping with a Tena-

> Young people need control and authority; and without it they are unhappy, confused, frustrated, and miserable. This is one of the psychological secrets that Hitler and Mussolini used so effectively in gaining control of the youth in Germany and Italy.
>
> BILLY GRAHAM

cious Teen who is desperate to garner control anywhere he or she can, be careful. If you overdo it on your dreams, on what matters most to you, he or she will view that as the target that's too easy to hit.

These are some of the most effective tools parents have in coping with a Tenacious Teen: Build a base of kindness, own your part in the problem, look for what's happening beneath the surface, critique with care, look for the good and affirm it, admit mistakes, be careful with rewards, don't be too positive, steer clear of regret, and don't make the target of rebellion too easy to hit. These are things that work. Put them into practice, and you will see just how effective they can be for your situation. However, it would be unfair for me to close this chapter without admitting something. You can do all the things I've talked about in this chapter and still have a terribly Tenacious Teenager on your hands. It's true. There are those cases in which very little seems to help. So, then what?

"They also serve who only stand and wait," said John Milton. Many times, breaking through a teenager's facade takes time and patience. After showering a teen with rays of personal warmth, owning your part of the problem, and critiquing with care and all the rest, sometimes little else can be done. It is important to recognize that in most cases, the Control Freak syndrome is only a phase for young people. Patience will help it pass. Simply waiting it out achieves more than forcing it out. As a Chinese proverb says: "With time and patience the mulberry leaf becomes silk."

PART 3

CONTROLLING
THE CONTROL FREAK
WITHIN

12

DIAGNOSING YOUR CONTROL FREAK SYMPTOMS

It is hard to fight an enemy who has outposts in your head.

SALLY KEMPTON

The scene is a newspaper office. The editor says to one of his reporters, "There's a fire raging out of control west of town, and I want you to get out there fast. And above all, get some good shots. If that means you have to hire an airplane, just do it. Don't worry about the expense."

The reporter, taking complete control of his assignment, called and ordered a plane. He rushed out to the airport, spotted a small aircraft with a young pilot in it, pulled open the door, jumped in, and ordered the pilot to take off. As directed, the pilot barreled down the runway and had just gotten the plane to a cruising altitude when the reporter said to him: "See that fire raging to the west? I want you to fly over that and get as close to the fire as we can."

Incredulous, the pilot replied, "You want me to fly over that fire?"

"Absolutely," the reporter said. "I'm a photojournalist, and I need dramatic shots of the fire!"

The pilot glanced over with a quizzical look on his face and said, "You mean you're not the flight instructor?"

If you're a Control Freak, you've probably felt like that reporter. Most Control Freaks can identify with how his command of the situation and his desire to get things quickly under control got him into trouble. I know I can. Just two years ago while vacationing in

Switzerland, I returned to my hotel room late one night after dinner to find that my camera had been stolen out of the luggage in my room. I knew exactly where I had left it, and it was gone. I also knew the housekeeper had taken it (we Control Freaks have a keen sense of being certain about things we haven't actually witnessed), and I was furious about losing not only the film with photos I'd taken all week but also an expensive camera.

Shot full of adrenaline, I ran downstairs to the main desk and demanded to speak to the hotel manager immediately (like most Control Freaks, I wanted action *now*). "I don't care if it's late, I want to speak to whoever is in charge," I gruffly told the desk clerk. A few minutes later a groggy manager appeared, and I told him my story and how I knew the housekeeper had taken the camera.

> A little kingdom I possess,
> Where thoughts and feelings dwell;
> And very hard the task I find
> Of governing it well.
>
> LOUISA MAY ALCOTT

"Are you sure you didn't take your camera with you to dinner, sir?" he asked me.

Give me a break, I thought to myself. *I've already solved the crime, and this guy is giving me the runaround.* "I think I'd know if I left my camera at the restaurant," I sarcastically snapped back.

That's when the manager's phone rang. It was the restaurant where I had eaten dinner that night. The owner was calling to see if any tourist in the hotel had mistakenly left an expensive camera behind.

THE HEART OF THE MATTER

Do you ever leap before you look? It's one of the many symptoms of Control Freak flu. We can be in such a hurry to get everything in our world under control that we make numerous mistakes in the process. Why? Because we feel *out* of control. That's the heart of the matter. Either we are trying not to feel out of control, or we are trying to avoid losing what little control we have. We run on a high-octane human fuel called anxiety. It's the germ that causes Control Freak flu. And once it spreads, anxiety manifests itself in a myriad of ways. Let me ask you a few questions that will also serve as examples of how anxiety may rear its head in your life.

Are you racing to get control of your time-starved life? Think about your breathless pace. Many Control Freaks tear into their days, trying to do more than is humanly possible in twenty-four hours—all in an attempt to get everything (tasks, schedules, money, etc.) under control. If you have a pressure-packed schedule that is driven by unending demands and deadlines, your probability of being a Control Freak rises.

> Anxiety is the natural result when our hopes are centered on anything short of God.
>
> BILLY GRAHAM

Are you too focused on the future? When I was a graduate student, I had this saying pinned up on the bulletin board above my desk for nearly five years: "Some people spend their entire lives indefinitely preparing to live." I stuck it there as a reminder to avoid thinking that real life begins after graduate school. It's a lesson most Control Freaks struggle to learn. We think, *Life begins after I get my promotion. Life begins when we move into our new house. Life begins when I finish this book.* The future, we want to believe, will be free from fretting. We'll have everything under control tomorrow. It's a tempting focus for those of us trying to keep anxiety at bay.

Do you sometimes overreact? You gain two pounds, for example, so you hardly eat for three days. Or maybe a slight change in schedule throws you into a panic. These are signs that anxiety is at work, and as a consequence, you're feeling out of control.

Do you lose perspective by playing the what-if game? Becoming obsessed with solving a potential problem— like suspecting that something is going wrong in a relationship or that you may be getting a less than stunning job-performance review—is a sign that you are in a control crisis and that you may be losing perspective on every-

> Can all your worries add a single moment to your life? Of course not!
>
> LUKE 12:25

thing else. Control Freaks often ask themselves, *What if . . . ?* And this question sets off a series of scenarios we want to control but probably can't.

Is your self-talk negative? Do you berate yourself for not having done everything on your to-do list? Do you punish yourself if a project wasn't done to your satisfaction? Being a self-imposed taskmaster and getting hung up on perfectionism is another danger sign that you've entered the control zone. And once again, the root is anxiety.

> Do not look forward to what may happen tomorrow. . . . Either God will shield you from suffering or he will give you unfailing strength to bear it.
>
> FRANCIS OF SALES

Do you sometimes freak out when things don't go your way? Do you ever lose it? A principal symptom of overcontrol is experiencing extreme emotional distress when something doesn't go the way you want it to. You end up saying or doing things that you regret. Relationships get damaged. Perhaps that's what led devotional writer Oswald Chambers to write, "Fretfulness springs from a determination to get my own way."

These questions are just the tip of the anxiety iceberg. You may deal with your anxiety in countless other ways, but the more of these questions you answer yes to, the stronger the probability is that you are suffering from symptoms of being a Control Freak. The true test, of course, is to assess whether your ways of coping with anxiety are interfering with your functioning. To do this, I suggest you take a moment to complete the following self-assessment.

THE CONTROL FREAK SELF-TEST

By answering the following multiple-choice questions, you can diagnose your own controlling symptoms. Circle the letter of the response that best represents your reaction. Take as much time as you like, and answer each question honestly.

1. Some of the items on my lengthy to-do list could be delegated to a family member or a coworker, but
   a. I don't ask anyone because I don't want to impose.
   b. I feel kind of awkward about it, but I eventually let people know I need help.
   c. I don't hesitate to ask people for help.
   d. I don't see the point of asking, because hardly anyone can do the job as well as I can do it myself.

2. My family members, friends, and coworkers tell me I am sometimes critical and hard to please.
   a. Never
   b. Sometimes
   c. Frequently
   d. All the time

3. When I've taken the time to make plans for an evening with friends and then they want to change what I have arranged,
   a. I don't say a word about it and am happy to go along without making a fuss.
   b. I let them know my feelings, but I eventually change my attitude and go along with it.
   c. I make it clear how hard I worked to pull everything together and try to convince them to see why my way is better.
   d. I make my stance known and don't budge.

4. When I'm having a disagreement with a sales clerk,
   a. I swallow my words and give in just to avoid the conflict.
   b. I work to resolve it as quickly as I can.
   c. I fight for my point even if it takes some time.
   d. I often go to the mat to win and show why I'm right.

5. When I'm in a hurry and the driver in front of me is driving especially slowly, causing me to miss green lights,
   a. I take that time to slow down and enjoy the ride.
   b. I hope he turns off the road so I can get going.
   c. I get very frustrated and do whatever I can to pass him.
   d. I ride his bumper, flash my lights or honk, and give him a dirty look when I get around him.

6. I'm taking a long-overdue vacation with a few friends. When it comes to making travel arrangements and planning our days, my style is to
   a. Let my friends do the planning and go with the flow.
   b. Offer a couple of suggestions but remain spontaneous.
   c. Think through things, like where we will want to eat on that day, and plan accordingly.
   d. Read up on where we are going, schedule each day ahead of time, and purchase tickets well in advance to avoid potential hassles.

7. In thinking about how people succeed in life,
   a. I go with the flow and see what happens.
   b. I think it's good to have goals, but everyone has his or her own style.
   c. I don't understand people who don't have vision for what they can do.
   d. I have little patience for those who simply drift without direction.

8. I just spent twenty minutes at the office doing absolutely nothing. I feel
   a. Justified. I deserve some slack-off time.
   b. Energized. It felt good to veg out.
   c. Grumpy. I could have finished a project and not felt so bad.

d. Guilty. I wasted precious time in which I could have gotten more done.

9. When someone borrows a video from my neatly organized collection and doesn't put the video back in the right order,
   a. It doesn't bother me.
   b. I'm just happy the person returned it.
   c. I put the video back the way I want it and make a mental note to tell the person where I like it to go.
   d. I show the person how to do it right and say that the next time he or she borrows a video, I want it returned to the exact place I have it.

10. When an important project I've been working on is not going the way I want it to,
    a. I shrug it off because nothing is really that important.
    b. I do something else and come back to the situation with a clear mind.
    c. I mull over the problem but do my best to leave my worries at work.
    d. I can't let it go. I worry to the point that it keeps me up at night.

11. When it comes to paying the bills in our home,
    a. I don't have anything to do with it.
    b. It doesn't matter who does it as long as it gets done.
    c. I do it myself if time allows or review the job if it was done by someone else to be sure I know what's going on.
    d. I always do it myself because I want to know exactly where our money is going, and I want to be sure the bills are paid on time.

12. I'm reading a book on being a Control Freak because
    a. Someone gave it to me. I'm not sure why.

b. I am primarily concerned with finding ways to cope with the overcontrolling people around me. But if reading the book keeps me from being controlling, that's great too.

c. I know that I have controlling tendencies and hope the book might help me improve.

d. I read through a few parts I think are best—just to be in the know—and don't give much weight to ideas I disagree with.

Scoring: Give yourself one point for every *A* you circled, two for every B, three for every *C*, and four for every *D*. Use the following information to interpret your total score:

Score of 13 or fewer: You aren't anywhere close to being a Control Freak. In fact, you may benefit from taking a course on assertiveness training.

Score of 14–22: You are probably pretty easygoing and rarely battle the Control Freak within.

Score of 23–35: You certainly have some Control Freak symptoms and can be diagnosed with occasional Control Freak flare-ups. The following chapters will help you inoculate yourself from the condition.

Score of 36–48: It's undeniable. You have a full-blown case of Control Freak flu and can clearly benefit from the prescription found in the remaining chapters of this book.

Now that you have pinpointed the severity of your tendency to overcontrol and have identified the degree to which it may be interfering with your functioning, let me give you an idea of what the remainder of this part of the book can do for you. The next three chapters will help you begin the process of controlling the

Control Freak within. First, I'll show you how to set some important safeguards to keep you from spinning out of control. We'll then follow that up with one of the most important things a recovering Control Freak can do—rebuild relationships that have been damaged from overcontrol. And finally, we will explore some of the most practical ways of taking charge without being an obnoxious Control Freak.

Worry is an indication that we think God cannot look after us.

OSWALD CHAMBERS

13

SAFEGUARDS TO KEEP YOU FROM
SPINNING OUT OF CONTROL

*Why do you hasten to remove anything that hurts your eye, while if
something affects your soul, you postpone the cure until next year?*

HORACE

One of the most famous homes in America was built just a
few miles from where I live in Seattle. It is perched on a six-
hundred-acre tract along the shore of Lake Washington and
has a spectacular, sweeping view of the Seattle skyline and the
snow-capped Olympic Mountains. At a cost of well over $50
million, it is no surprise that people are talking. It is the house
Bill Gates built.

And it's no surprise that this high-tech Control Freak went to
outrageous lengths to control his environment. For example, the
home has no visible electrical outlets anywhere because Gates
does not like "clutter." The seventy-foot-tall wood columns that
support the roof in the entry area are similar to large logs in a
lodge except the logs were specially sanded to create a "perfect"
satin finish. In fact, all timbers throughout the home are nearly
"flawless" in that they have no knots. And all of the bolts throughout the house are stainless steel and are oriented in the same
direction.

Gates felt that an existing cedar tree on the property was not
located in the right place and had the entire tree moved six inches.
Like other trees on the compound, it is monitored electronically
twenty-four hours a day via computer, so if the soil around it gets
dry, it gets just the right amount of water. And so does Gates. His

master bathtub can be filled to the right temperature and precise depth by Gates as he drives home from work. Just another day in the life of the world's richest Control Freak.

Truth is, if you and I had the resources of Bill Gates, we would most likely ratchet up our control quotient too. Who wouldn't want a flawless home with the convenience of heated floors and driveways, a state-of-the-art home theater, and all the rest?

Even for the lowly computer illiterate, a flood of new technology means we have much more control over things we never imagined. But along with the convenience technology brings also comes an increased demand to maintain control. We can instantly send E-mail to people on the other side of the globe, for example, but we also feel compelled to check and recheck our messages throughout the day to keep current.

> He that would govern others, first should be the master of himself.
>
> PHILIP MASSINGER

What is a Control Freak to do? With so many modern ways to maintain "control," how can we keep from going overboard? This chapter is devoted to giving you several tips for doing just that. In no particular order, here are some of the most effective ways to keep your controlling tendencies from spinning out of control.

SLOW DOWN

All of us live time-starved lives. We complain about how busy we are, but these complaints too often sound more like pride than protests. We equate busyness with being important. Ask any doctor—if he or she has the time. A recent study found that physicians don't have time to listen. Patients usually have an average of four questions to ask on a typical visit, but it turns out that during the appointment time, they are able to ask just one or two. Once a patient starts speaking, the first interruption by the physician occurs, on average, within eighteen seconds.[1] This is not a problem exclusive to doctors, of course. All of us suffer from hurry sickness. It's part of taking control. So, keeping your inner Control Freak in check means that you will have to slow down.

Do you find yourself growing impatient when someone takes too long to finish a story? Do you tear into your to-do list at a breathless pace? Chances are you need to push the pause button, step off the hamster wheel, and catch your breath. Unwind. It's the only sure cure for a case of cranky control.

> A candle loses nothing by lighting another candle.
>
> PROVERB

REDUCE YOUR ANXIETY LEVEL

"Anxiety," said playwright William Inge, "is the interest paid on trouble before it is due." What does your interest rate look like? Chances are it's far too high. To tame the Control Freak within, you need to do whatever you can to reduce your level of anxiety. For some people, a soothing bath helps take the edge off. For others, it's a relaxing massage. Some find relief through exercise. All of these things and plenty more are helpful to the anxious person, but the real cure lies much deeper.

At the root of all anxiety is a bewildering and sometimes terrifying feeling of being out of control. And I am convinced that if we are to ever control this feeling of being out of control, it will be because we have faith. For me, that means believing and trusting that God is in control. Whenever I feel myself spinning helplessly out of control with anxiety, I know it is because I have lost faith. I love what British prayer warrior George Müller had to say about anxiety: "The beginning of anxiety is the end of faith; and the beginning of true faith is the end of anxiety." I know of few messages more pertinent for the recovering Control Freak.

> If you don't get everything you want, think of the things you don't get that you don't want.
>
> OSCAR WILDE

GRIT YOUR TEETH AND DELEGATE

Yes, I know. It's truly astonishing how incompetent other people can be. They not only don't do things as well as you do, they can't do them as quickly. So, like a good little Control Freak, you do it yourself—sometimes even after you've asked someone else to do it!

Most Control Freaks live by this adage: If you want something done right, do it yourself. Nevertheless, if you want to keep your controlling ways in check, you've got to learn to delegate. Sure, there are those jobs you may not trust to anyone else, but give other people a chance to do projects that don't require perfection. And once you do so, take a deep breath and live with the job they do. Don't critique it, amend it, correct it, improve it, upgrade it, or in any other way put your stamp on it. Look for the good they have done, not the bad. In other words, show some respect. This will take an extra ounce of self-discipline, but the more you do it, the more relaxed you will become. You'll discover that you don't have to carry the responsibility alone. You'll be surprised how nice it feels not to be in charge all the time.

> God particularly pours out his blessings upon those who know how much they need him.
>
> ROBERT H. SCHULLER

GIVE UP THE "IF ONLYS"

I was on a lecture tour in Australia a couple years ago and learned an important lesson from the Australian coat of arms. I was admiring this intriguing crest when I asked my host about the meaning of its depiction of the emu and the kangaroo. "Emus and kangaroos cannot walk backward," he said. He went on to tell me that it's a continual reminder to Australians that their country is not focused on the past.

Most recovering Control Freaks would benefit from having a similar reminder on their family coat of arms. After all, it's so tempting for those of us who want everything under perfect control to dwell on disappointments and be filled with regrets. "If only I would have . . ." But keeping controlling behaviors under control requires a release of these inner demons. When you find yourself saying, "If only . . . ," allow yourself to be human, make a few mistakes, and move on. Don't walk backward.

DEFER TO OTHERS WHENEVER YOU CAN

We Control Freaks are notorious for stepping over other people's ideas and opinions. We know what we want and aren't afraid to make our wants known. And because we are not afraid to voice our wants, we sometimes don't even notice when others are doing the same.

I was picked up from the airport by people who were serving as my hosts for a speaking engagement. I slipped into the backseat of their car. The husband was driving, and his wife sat in the front passenger side. Since we had some spare time before the evening's event, the husband asked if I'd like to grab a bite to eat on the way to the auditorium. "Sure," I said, "anything but Chinese food. I had that for lunch."

> Do all the good you can,
> By all the means you can,
> In all the ways you can,
> In all the places you can,
> At all the times you can,
> To all the people you can,
> As long as ever you can.
>
> JOHN WESLEY

"I know just the place," the man replied. Ten minutes later we pulled into the parking lot of a Chinese restaurant.

"Honey," the man's wife stated, "Dr. Parrott said he didn't want Chinese." The man turned off the car and said, "Oh, he's going to like this Chinese food. I've been wanting to eat here for weeks."

It was almost unfathomable. Was I in the Twilight Zone? I made one request to this man, and he didn't seem to even care. The experience got me thinking about how often I'm not the most sensitive to other people's desires. I hope I've never been as rude as my host was on this occasion, but I can assure you that it's sometimes a struggle for me to defer to others. Chances are it's a struggle for you too. Make a habit not only of asking people for their ideas and opinions but also of actually listening to what they say. It's the uncontrolling thing to do.

LEARN THE CLEANING LADY'S NAME

A professor gave a pop quiz with several questions. The last one read: "What is the first name of the woman who cleans the school?" Was it some kind of joke? Why would this be counted as information students needed to know? None of the students could answer the last question, and one student asked if the answer would be counted in the test grade. "Absolutely," said the professor. "In your careers you will meet many people. All are significant. They deserve your attention and care, even if all you do is smile and say hello." The students never forgot that lesson. And they learned to say hello to Dorothy, the cleaning lady.

This is an important lesson for all of us who want to keep from being a Control Freak. Why? Because our desire to accomplish our tasks, and thus gain more control, forces us to wear blinders that keep us from seeing people whom we think don't matter. It's a sure sign of someone spinning out of control. And learning the cleaning lady's name is a sure way to keep from falling.

> I use not only all the brains I have but all I can borrow.
>
> WOODROW WILSON

BE NEITHER PUSHY NOR A PUSHOVER

In working with people who are trying to change their controlling tendencies, I've seen some sincere people do a terrible about-face. Suddenly, they become doormats. They give in to everyone else's opinions and never articulate their own. Where they once only demanded, they now only give. They give so much that they eventually give up their identity and then wonder why they feel so empty.

In your journey toward becoming a less controlling person, don't cut off parts of your personality. You are obviously a strong person. And granted, maybe you sometimes come on a little too strong. But chances are that the people who know you the best don't want you to become Caspar Milquetoast. As someone recently told me, "I'm just trying to turn down the volume, but I'm not going to quit playing my music." She understood that the goal here is to be neither pushy nor a pushover.

> Let not thy will roar when thy power can but whisper.
>
> SIR THOMAS FULLER

KNOW WHERE YOU CAN—AND CAN'T—EXERT INFLUENCE

Anyone who knew Walt Disney knew he was a Control Freak. He forbade men with long hair to enter the gates of Disneyland. And he was furious when he realized he couldn't do anything to stop the bars, sleazy motels, and strip clubs from sprouting up alongside his 244-acre Magic Kingdom. One day Disney had a Donald Duck–style temper tantrum because of this and swore he would build another Magic Kingdom where he could control its environs. Disney World was the result. Most of us do not have the resources to control our environment as Walt Disney did. But that doesn't keep us from trying.

I know of a department-store manager who nearly lost his marriage because he was treating his wife like an employee. He would order her around the home, never asking for her advice or input. If you want to keep your controlling tendencies from getting out of control, you have to decide where you can exert your influence and where you can't.

DO ONE THING AT A TIME

Multitasking is a favorite pastime of most Control Freaks. Let's be honest, it feels good to get more done in less time. Why? Because it helps us feel more in control, less anxious. So we scan E-mail while we're talking to someone on the phone. We brush our teeth while watching CNN. We glance at the sports page while driving to work and listening to the radio and eating a donut, all at the same time. *I must be in control. Look at all I'm getting done,* we think to ourselves.

The problem with multitasking is that it takes a toll on relationships. Most multitaskers admit that it increases the chances of making mistakes and that it may even lead to overload and burnout. But the real problem surfaces in the breakdown in communication with our families and coworkers. Multitasking pushes them out of the picture. They become just one more thing to take

> Two captains in one boat make it sink.
>
> ARABIAN PROVERB

care of. When you're doing business on the phone, for example, while mouthing silent messages to someone else in the room, don't even think about that as true communication. And don't think you can carry on a conversation with someone you love while reading a magazine or newspaper. What you do, not just what you say, sends a strong message to the people you are with. So consider doing one thing at a time— for their sake as well as your own.

LEARN TO BE LED RATHER THAN LEAD

Another good safeguard to keep you from spinning out of control with your controlling ways is to put yourself in places where you simply have very little control. Now, I'm not talking about putting yourself in danger. I'm talking about doing something that enables you to be led rather than taking the lead. One of the best ways of doing that is to pick up a new hobby or sport and then to put yourself in someone else's hands to teach you.

Chuck was a commanding Control Freak who rarely ventured into areas where he was not in charge. During the time Chuck was a client of mine, I gave him an assignment to find an activity for which he would have to rely on others. I never imagined that he would take up mountain climbing. But he did. He told me how he joined a climbing club in which an instructor told *him* what to do. "It's terrific," he told me. "When I'm tethered to another climber and scaling a wall, I have to depend on that person. It's teaching me so much about myself."

In the same way, unpredictable environments can help Control Freaks win over their out-of-control behavior. Sometimes Control Freaks become so obsessed with control that they no longer venture into areas that may require them to give up command. So take the risk. Don't be afraid of places where you are not in charge.

COUNT YOUR BLESSINGS

On a personal note, the best advice I ever received on my road to recovery from being a Control Freak was from my father. As a retired college president with many years of knowing what it's like to be in charge as well as to have fun, my dad sat me down as an adult child and asked me a question: "Why are you driving so hard, Son?" My knee-jerk response was a joke: "To keep up with you, Dad." He thought I was serious. We talked about the psychological pressure that is transmitted, intentionally or not, from one generation to the next. We talked about the drive to produce and our mutual compulsions for control. Then my dad told me his secret for keeping life under control without being a Control Freak. "Count your blessings," he said. "Don't let a day slip away without taking time to appreciate God's gifts."

> One of the marks of true greatness is the ability to develop greatness in others.
>
> J. C. MACAULAY

It was a few years ago that my dad and I had that conversation. But I haven't forgotten. And I've discovered he's right. When I take time to appreciate the blessings I enjoy, the things I'm trying desperately to control usually pale by comparison.

Now that you have read through my suggestions for preventing your controlling tendencies from getting out of control, I fear one of two things may have happened. First, I fear you may have looked over the list and thought, *That's too tough. I can't do all those things.* If that's the case, I urge you simply to zero in on one or two of these things and work on them for a while. Once you begin to get a handle on these one or two things, come back to the list and try some more.

My other fear—in fact it is a stronger one—is that you will read through this list, put each of these things on your to-do list, and launch a full attack. In other words, you will become overcontrolling in your attempt to get control of your controlling compulsions. I fear you will channel the very controlling behavior you are trying to overcome toward the things that can help you do so. If this is your temptation, I urge you to heed the advice of my first step and slow down. You need to take your time as you try to change what is probably a pretty entrenched way of being for you.

Also, you need to keep the big picture in mind: Anxiety is what fuels control. Motivational speaker Arthur Somers Roche said it well: "Anxiety is a thin stream of fear trickling through the mind. If encouraged, it cuts a channel into which all other thoughts are drained." Beware as you tame the Control Freak within. Don't allow your old habits to cloud the process. And take courage too. The more you do to soothe your anxious soul, the more you and your relationships will find a space to be at peace.

> A person who is to be happy must actively enjoy his blessings.
>
> CICERO

14

REBUILDING YOUR RELATIONSHIPS

The only person you can control is yourself.

MARIAN WRIGHT EDELMAN

Denise took pride in how well she juggled a husband, two grade-schoolers, and a demanding job—and still managed to make time for aerobics, a gourmet-cooking class, and gardening. It was largely because of her ability to handle so many things so well that her marriage was solid and that her kids were so normal.

Sure, she could be a little overbearing at times, but she dreaded the embarrassments she believed she, her family, and her employer would suffer if they couldn't keep all their lives moving in the right direction. She ran a tight ship, and it was for the best—or so she thought.

Then, on Denise and William's twelfth anniversary, they had one of the worst fights of their marriage. Two weeks earlier their closest friends had offered to take them out to celebrate. Denise said she'd rather make dinner for everyone so she could try out some new recipes. But William didn't want to go to all that trouble. "They want to do something for us. Why can't we just let them?" he asked. It was decided they would definitely go out to dinner.

It wasn't a happy dinner. Concerned about the kids, Denise called the baby-sitter twice, then suggested that she and William skip dessert and leave. On the way home, William expressed his disappointment with the evening. She told him he was insensitive. "Why does everything have to go your way?" he yelled. Rarely one to launch a personal attack, William gave a final blow: "You're nothing short of a Control Freak."

They rode the rest of the way home in silence. William was fuming, but Denise was doing some serious soul searching. It wasn't the first time she had been told she was overpowering.

THE RELATIONAL RESULTS OF COMPULSIVE CONTROL

Nothing suffers more from overcontrol than our relationships. And these days we can't afford to do them too much damage. National surveys find that a quarter of all Americans say they've felt lonely in the last month.[1] And as any self-confessed Control Freak will tell you, trying to control other people does nothing if not push them further away.

Denise, like most Control Freaks, didn't want to hurt her husband. But in her attempts to control her own anxiety, she ended up trying to control him and everyone else in her life. Let's make this clear: At the root of all controlling behavior is an attempt to tame our anxiety—not to dominate another person. That's why control is so tempting.

> He who cannot forgive another breaks the bridge over which he must pass himself.
>
> GEORGE HERBERT

It is intensely seductive. Control tickles our psyches with a sense of peace and calm. It provides us with a delicious taste of power over everything that seems beyond real control, namely time and other people. As a result, many of us end up fighting simply to achieve that powerful control, both when it's appropriate (how you like to spend your birthday) and when it's not (how others ought to spend theirs). For the true Control Freak, compromise just doesn't seem as gratifying as an out-and-out victory, and that makes it easy to forget that your triumph represents someone else's defeat. The result: Relationships get damaged.

And lest you think that controlling tendencies damage only home-front relationships, I want to introduce you to Randy. He's the president of a large real estate firm, and he keeps his staff "under control" by creating an air of mystery and uncertainty about company policies. His employees never know for sure if they will have a job the next week, so they stay alert to any hints the boss gives out. "Sure, he keeps people under control," says one of his top-producing sales people, "but the competent people won't stand for it. I'm quitting."

> The formula for achieving a successful relationship is simple: you should treat all disasters as if they were trivialities, but never treat a triviality as if it were a disaster.
>
> QUENTIN CRISP

No one can claim that trying to control other people does not work at some level. But let's look at what it really means for us to "succeed" at controlling another person. Randy gained a feeling of power and importance, but he lost the base of his productivity: a competent, self-respecting sales staff. When we try to manipulate or control others, we might win at one level, but we invariably lose at several others.

Whether the relationships you need to repair are at home or in the workplace, the following suggestions may prove helpful.

A THREE-POINT PLAN FOR REPAIRING RELATIONSHIPS

It would be absurd for me to think that every damaged relationship could be restored with "three easy steps." I don't even begin to think in those terms. However, after years of working with people to mend the relationships that matter most, I have come to believe that every relationship—those in pain and those in pleasure—can benefit significantly from a generous supply of grace.

Why grace? Because it offers the gift of being accepted before we are acceptable. Grace doesn't demand perfection; it doesn't manipulate or cajole. Grace frees the spirit to let go and let be.

> All men who live with any degree of serenity live by some assurance of grace.
>
> REINHOLD NIEBUHR

Maybe you can identify with Hank, a Control Freak trying to improve his relationships but not knowing how. For years, Hank has kept his children under tight control by regulating their supply of money. "I'd like to leave

Kansas City and move to Chicago," says his twenty-eight-year-old daughter, "but Daddy wouldn't stand for it." She could spend hours telling you how she feels obligated to her father, how she does whatever he tells her to do. "I know she's a grown woman," Hank says about his daughter, "but I really want her to stay where she has some roots." When pressed, however, Hank confesses that his real motivation is to keep her close by because it's better for him, not her. A gentle thumb in his daughter's back helps Hank maintain control and temporarily elude his anxiety.

Whom do you feel most sorry for in this scenario? Hank or his daughter? I'm torn. I don't know whether to feel most sorry for the daughter for allowing herself to be co-opted or for her father, who is unknowingly destroying an important relationship because of his control issues. If forced to decide, I would have to say the father. Like most Control Freaks, he loses, whether or not he knows it. Have you discovered this in your own life yet?

> Grace is Christianity's best gift to the world, a spiritual nova in our midst exerting a force stronger than vengeance.
>
> PHILIP YANCEY

They say that the man who pays the piper calls the tune, but in personal relationships, what's the pleasure in calling the tune? Where's the joy in being in charge? Where's the respect in sharing ideas? Where's the grace? When we try to control other people, we certainly hurt those people, but most of all we cheat ourselves. That's why our relationships, from all sides, are crying out for grace.

If you want to rebuild your relationships that have been damaged by overcontrol, here's my proposal: Ask for grace, give grace, and receive grace.

Ask for Grace

"I had a friend, Katherine, who was always late," said Jamie, a young professional woman who was generally upbeat and gregarious. "No matter what time we were supposed to meet, Katherine would waltz in twenty to thirty minutes later. After a while I resented it because I realized that it was her way of trying to control me—Katherine made me wait until it was convenient for her to arrive. It really bothered me, but I never had the nerve to confront her. Finally I just stopped seeing Katherine altogether."

This is the irony of most manipulative ploys: They may help us keep other people under control temporarily, but in the end they make us lose them altogether. That's why every recovering Control Freak needs to ask others for grace. It is a crucial step to repairing the relational damage we do with our controlling ways. And it's the most humiliating step too.

> There's only one corner of the universe you can be certain of improving, and that's your own self.
>
> ALDOUS HUXLEY

Maybe you have a former friend like Jamie, someone whom you used to enjoy being with but who gave up on you because you damaged the relationship with controlling behavior. If so, you can hang all hope of healing the relationship on grace. Once you ask for grace from that person, you open the possibility for a renewed relationship, one that will be nourished by forgiveness and strengthened by mercy.

Katherine took this daring step when she phoned Jamie at her home. "I'd love to do this in person, Jamie," Katherine said, "but I know I'd be pressing my luck to ask for that. Anyway, I want to apologize for what I did to our relationship. I don't know if I knew it then, but I know it now—I was a jerk. I'm so sorry for taking you for granted and thinking my schedule was more important than yours. I wouldn't blame you if you never wanted to get together with me again. I would understand. But I'm asking you to give me another chance. I'm asking you for grace. I know I don't deserve it. But I'm asking because I value you and our relationship."

> The highest pact we can make with our fellow is— "Let there be truth between us two forevermore."
>
> RALPH WALDO EMERSON

Let's face it. It's tough for anyone, let alone Control Freaks, to admit they haven't been the kind of person they want to be. But this courageous step of asking friends and family for forgiveness and grace, just as Katherine did, will clear the way for a fresh start and a restored relationship. It sends a signal that you are serious about relinquishing control over that person. And it says you may need that person's forgiveness when you fail. Most of all, it says you value and respect the person and your relationship.

Give Grace

Through a mental trick called projection, we begin to think, *It's not me that needs to manage my anger; it's you.* Or we may think, *It's not me that needs to quit gossiping; it's you.* This projection of our own experience onto others allows us to "fix" *them* without acknowledging that the problem is in *us.*

> O momentary grace of mortal men,
> Which we more hunt for than the grace of God.
>
> WILLIAM SHAKESPEARE

As a professor, I sometimes feel myself losing patience with a student who shows up at my office on the day of registration saying, "Do you know what classes I should take next term?" I briskly turn to the university time schedule and matter-of-factly plan the student's projected course schedule. All the while I am resenting the time I'm sacrificing to do something the student should have started to do himself. I make it clear to the student that I will not be planning every semester for him. He has to take control.

> The growth of grace is like the polishing of metals. There is first an opaque surface; by and by you see a spark darting out, then a strong light; till at length it sends back a perfect image of the sun that shines upon it.
>
> EDWARD PAYSON

But over the years of advising disorganized or slacker students, I have discovered that I am often just like them. Not that I am disorganized or unmotivated, but part of me is more than happy to relinquish my responsibilities to others if they are in a position to help me. Why should I make my flight reservations for a speaking engagement when the host organization can do it for me? Why should I do the hard work of editing this paragraph if my editor is paid to do it for me? The point is, at times, I can be just like the students who push my buttons. And that's why they irritate me.

These students remind me of the part of myself I don't like. They show me my dark side, so I project it right back.

Chances are you do the same. If there's a behavior that you find yourself constantly trying to control in other people, consider whether it is something you have not confronted or resolved in yourself. As long as you have not controlled that aspect of yourself, it is likely to be a source of supreme annoyance to you when other people do it. And that's why you need to give them grace.

Receive Grace

One of the most influential professors in my graduate training was Dr. Lewis Smedes. He and I talked one day in his office about some research I was doing on the emotion of guilt. "Les, sometimes I feel vaguely guilty," he confessed to me as a student, "but I don't know of anything in particular to feel guilty about." Lew often shocked me with his vulnerability. I don't know why. I should have been used to it from reading his amazingly transparent books. In fact it was in one of his books that Lew eventually solved the mystery of his emotional puzzle.

"Guilt was not my problem as I felt it," he writes in *Shame and Grace*. "What I felt most was a glob of unworthiness that I could not tie down to any concrete sins I was guilty of. What I needed more than pardon was a sense that God accepted me, owned me, held me, affirmed me, and would never let go of me even if he was not too much impressed with what he had on his hands."[2] This was Lew's way of coming to terms with his need for grace. A desperate need we all share.

> That is the mystery of grace: it never comes too late.
>
> FRANÇOIS MAURIAC

Ultimately, the rebuilding of our relationships rests, I am convinced, with a spiritual experience—to be more specific, a spiritual experience of grace from God. Because the web of control we use to entrap other people is woven so tightly with tangled threads of existential anxiety, we need God's amazing grace to free us. We need God's grace to sink deep down into our hearts and loosen our fearful fists from around our compulsive need to control the things we never really can.

Before we go much further, I need to explain that grace is not a magic pill we swallow to make our relationships better. Its purpose is not to cure Control Freaks. Grace, for the most part, is the experience of being accepted. As my friend Lew would say, grace is the discovery that we are accepted by the grace of the One whose acceptance of us matters most.

When we receive God's grace, we receive the balm that soothes the anxious soul. We realize we are accepted with no possibility of being rejected. Accepted once and forever. Accepted at the ultimate depth of our being. We are given what we have longed for in every nuance of every relationship.

Grace comes free of charge to people who do not deserve it, and I am one of those people. I am trying in my own way to sing a song of grace by asking for it, giving it as best I can, and receiving it at every turn. I do so because I know that the rebuilding of broken relationships rests solely on grace. I do so because I know, more surely than I know anything else, that we are all saved by grace.

Once again, I urge you to ask for grace, give grace, and receive grace.

15

HOW TO TAKE CHARGE WITHOUT
BEING A CONTROL FREAK

None of us are as smart as all of us.

JAPANESE PROVERB

The great spiritual writer Henri Nouwen's final book before he died in 1996 was a diary of his last year. Throughout his journal he talks about the Flying Rodleighs, trapeze artists. He was touched by their skill and grace on the trapeze. Much of his attraction to their circus performance had to do with the special relationship between the flyer and the catcher. Swinging high above the crowd, the daredevil flyer lets go of the trapeze simply to stretch out his arms and wait to feel the strong hands of the catcher pluck him out of the air. "The flyer must never catch the catcher," Rodleigh had told him. "He must wait in absolute trust."[1]

What a powerful message for those of us who are driven by control. Can you imagine the strong-minded discipline it takes to surrender your own efforts to the hands of another? To fly helpless through the air and yet resist your internal compulsion for control? To rely solely on someone else to save you?

This kind of trust seems beyond comprehension to most of us. Yet it is the very quality that will save us from ourselves. Trust is what propels us beyond being overly opinionated, intrusive, tenacious, domineering, invasive, and impatient.

Before you fear this final chapter is a call to surrender all control, relax. All we're talking about is how to remain in charge without being a cranky Control Freak. After all, *influencing* other people is not the same as *controlling* them. The difference is that people who are trying to control others have little respect for the judgment and autonomy of the people they are trying to control— while people who can influence others know others can think for themselves and respect people's ability to make their own decisions. In other words, they know how to trust. They have faith, if only a little, in the other people.

This final chapter, therefore, is dedicated to helping you cultivate that quality. To put it plainly, this chapter will show you how to maintain your influence without being obnoxious. It will help you give direction without being a dictator.

> Let no one ever come to you without leaving better and happier.
>
> MOTHER TERESA

Whether you are a parent, a friend, a spouse, or a coworker, I leave you with a short, simple, yet difficult, message for helping you become the kind of person you want to be. And in a sense, part of that message is to focus on that very thing—not on what you *do* but on who you *are*.

A TRANSFORMING TRUTH

For most recovering Control Freaks, trusting another person to oversee an important project makes about as much sense as trusting a rabbit to deliver a head of lettuce. It's downright difficult to give up the control that trust demands. So how does one do it?

It begins when we allow a sobering truth to seep deep into our spirit: *God gave us the power to imagine the future but gave us no power to control it.* We can imagine good things that we *want* to happen, but we cannot see to it that they *will* happen. We can also imagine bad things that we do not want to happen, but we cannot see to it that they won't happen.

Life, by its very definition, is uncertain. Uncontrollable. These are tough words, I understand. But this very truth is the message we need most to hear. For the more we mortals believe we can control our little worlds, the more we delude ourselves into thinking we are gods. And that's a mistake no one can afford to make.

Life is uncertain. When the truth of this message sinks in, it transforms the soul of control. It loosens our clinched grip on those things and those people we are trying so desperately to direct. I'll say it again: this transforming truth shows us that life is not so much about what we *do* but about who we *are*. It shows us that we are mere mortals who cannot control much of anything in this uncertain world. This truth takes us to a new vista where we see that the only peace that can be enjoyed on this planet is found in the faith and trust and grace we give to each other. And ultimately our faith in God and his grace is what gives us the serenity to change those few things over which we have control (especially our attitude) and accept those things over which we don't. This transforming truth is what allows us to relinquish our compulsion for control to the only One who is in control.

> Why are we so full of restraint? Why do we not give in all directions? Is it fear of losing ourselves? Until we do lose ourselves, there is no hope of finding ourselves.
>
> HENRY MILLER

PUTTING THE TRANSFORMING TRUTH INTO PRACTICE

Near the beginning of this chapter I promised to show you how to maintain your influence without being obnoxious. Let me put the transforming truth I just talked about into practical terms. Understand, of course, that what I am about to share with you will make absolutely no difference in your life if it is not predicated on the transforming truth that life is uncertain and you can't control it. What I am about to give you assumes that you have internalized the fact that only God is in control. Once you have wrapped your mind around this truth, the following steps will help you live it out.

> Grace is love that cares and stoops and rescues.
>
> JOHN R. W. STOTT

It's not necessary for me to give you a long list of do's and don'ts. That only complicates the personal transformation you're trying to achieve. Instead, I offer three inoculations for curing your control freak flu: relinquish control on a daily basis; maximize others' potential; and admit when you're wrong.

Relinquish Control

If you're sincere about giving up your Control Freak ways, and I believe you are or you wouldn't be reading this chapter, you've got to make a habit out of relinquishing control. And the best way to make anything a habit is to build into your life daily reminders and patterns that cause you to do that behavior so often that you no longer even think about it. It becomes second nature. It's habit.

I have a friend, a self-confessed Control Freak in recovery, who starts most mornings with a quiet moment of meditation. He holds his hands in front of him, palms up, and prays for God to take away whatever he is trying to hold on to. It takes him only a brief moment, but it sets the tone for his day. I know another person who makes a mental note to relinquish his control before he goes into a conference room at work. He knows this is where he tends to be most controlling, so he always pauses before entering to be sure he leaves his controlling tendencies at the door. Once inside the room, he writes the word *relinquish* at the top of his legal pad in front of him. I know a mom who is trying to become less controlling with her kids. She uses the mailbox outside their house as a mental reminder to leave her control there as she drives up the driveway.

> What is faith? It is the confident assurance that what we hope for is going to happen. It is the evidence of things we cannot yet see.
>
> HEBREWS 11:1

There are countless ways to remind yourself to relinquish control. Consider what might work for you, and begin seeing how this simple awareness can help you tame your control.

Maximize Others' Potential

Nurture. That's what this next principle is all about—nurturing other people's positive potential. I can almost hear some of you saying, "Nurture? That's not even in my vocabulary." You're right.

That's why it's so important that you begin to commit yourself to it. Actor Danny Thomas once said, "Success in life has nothing to do with what you gain in life or accomplish for yourself. It's what you do for others." It's a statement every recovering Control Freak would do well to memorize.

> O, it is excellent
> To have a giant's
> strength,
> but it is tyrannous
> To use it like a giant.
>
> WILLIAM SHAKESPEARE

You maximize other people's potential when you nurture their spirit. And you nurture another person's spirit when you encourage him or her. Encouraging words are the legs that nurture walks on. Celebrated UCLA basketball coach John Wooden told players who scored to give a smile or nod to the player who gave them a good pass. "What if he's not looking?" asked a team member. Wooden replied, "I guarantee he'll look." Everyone values encouragement and looks for it—especially from Control Freaks.

So what are you doing to encourage others around you? How are you maximizing other people's potential at work or at home? I'm sure you agree that nurturing a small child is important, but have you lost sight of the value of nurturing adults? Control Freaks often do. We assume adults will nurture themselves, right? We may even think it's a weakness to be nurtured. But if we want to influence others without being obnoxious, we've got to learn to nurture them. Each time we nurture other people, each time we give them some encouragement, we maximize their potential. And we become more and more influential ourselves in the process. As Ralph Waldo Emerson said, "It is one of the most beautiful

> It is impossible to go
> through life without trust:
> that is to be imprisoned
> in the worst cell of all,
> oneself.
>
> GRAHAM GREENE

compensations of this life that no man can sincerely try to help another without helping himself."

Admit When You're Wrong

What do you do when you know you're wrong? Be honest. Do you try to cover it up? Do you try to shift the blame? Do you make excuses? Do you hope no one notices and move on? These are a few of Control Freaks' favorite tactics when they discover they're wrong. And they are also some of the most obnoxious behaviors a Control Freak can do.

If you want to put the transforming truth into practice, you will need to admit your mistakes. Each time you do, you are saying, *I'm not in control. I'm fallible, but life goes on.* Admitting your mistakes is one of the quickest roads to dismantling your controlling tendencies because it will bring you straight to humility. The word *humility,* by the way, literally means "close to the ground." It conjures up an image of someone who is bowing—a posture foreign to most Control Freaks. But don't worry, I'm not asking you to do that. I'm simply suggesting that people of real influence admit when they are wrong and aren't afraid to say, "I'm sorry."

> God, our wise and creative Maker, has been pleased to make everyone different and no one perfect. The sooner we appreciate and accept that fact, the deeper we will appreciate and accept one another.
>
> CHARLES R. SWINDOLL

Here's what I suggest. If you know you are wrong, say about yourself all the derogatory things you know the other person is thinking or wants to say or intends to say. And if you say them before the other person has a chance to say them, you'll take the wind right out of his or her sail. "When I told you to take Interstate 5 instead of Highway 99 because there would be less traffic, I didn't figure on the new construction. You're probably thinking I'm a pompous know-it-all who thinks he has the answer to every traffic dilemma in the city. I obviously don't, and I'm sorry I made you late to your appointment." Get the idea? The chances are a hundred to one that the person you offended will take a generous, forgiving attitude and minimize your mistake.

I have a friend who is fond of saying, "Humble pie is a pastry that's never tasty." I tend to agree, but I think humility can be an acquired taste. Even so, I'm not asking you to enjoy the idea of admitting your mistakes and saying you're sorry, but I can assure you that the more often you do this, the more influence you will garner and the less obnoxious you'll become.

Well, that's it. Three things you can do to influence people without being obnoxious. One, relinquish control on a daily basis. This will help you become a healthier person. Two, maximize other people's potential with words of encouragement. This will help you increase your effectiveness with those around you. And, three, embrace humility by admitting when you're wrong. This will prevent you from developing hurtful relationships at work and at home.

> It is our uniqueness that gives freshness and vitality to a relationship.
>
> JAMES C. DOBSON

There's one more thought along these lines I'd like to leave you with. It is perhaps the best advice I know of for taking charge without being a Control Freak. I call it "the gift."

THE GIFT THAT MATTERS MOST

Anyone who has ever read Loren Eiseley's short story "The Star Thrower" has caught a glimpse into the secret of surrendering control and finding faith. It is the story of a young man who makes a trip to the ocean's shore to gain perspective on the meaning of life. At the beach, the young man notices dozens of tourists collecting shells. They are engaged in a kind of greedy madness to out-collect their less aggressive neighbors. He watches people scrambling along the beach at dawn with bundles of gathered starfish, hermit crabs, sea urchins, and other living shellfish. He watches them argue and topple over each other as they rush in a kind of frenzy to collect their souvenirs.

The young man then notices these hurried collectors gathered around a large outdoor kettle provided by the beachfront resort hotel as a service to its guests. They are dropping their shells, occupants included, into the boiling water and then retrieving the shells to show off to friends and relatives back home.

> No man is free who is not master of himself.
>
> EPICTETUS

About that time, the young man in the story also notices a solitary human figure, an old man, standing near the water's edge in the center of a rainbow caused by the sun-filled spray. The old man would stoop over, then stand up to fling an object out to sea beyond the breaking surf. As the young man watched the repeated motion of the old man, he finally walked toward him and asked what he was doing. The old man answered softly, "I'm a star thrower."

He once again reached down to pick up another starfish and, with a quick yet gentle movement, spun it gracefully far out into the sea. "It may live," he said, "if the offshore pull is strong enough."

The younger man thought for a moment, then silently reached down and skipped a still-living star across the water toward freedom. He looked back over his shoulder. Against the rainbow, the old star thrower stooped and flung once more. The younger man found the fresh perspective he was looking for.

And so will you, each time you give other people freedom to be who they really are, free from manipulation and overcontrol.

NOTES

CHAPTER 4—IS ALL CONTROL BAD?

1. Judith Rodin, "Control, Health, and Aging" (address given to the Society of Behavioral Medicine, Boston, Mass., 1988).
2. Martin Seligman, *Helplessness* (New York: W. H. Freeman, 1975), 46.
3. J. H. Johnson and I. G. Sarason, "Life Stress, Depression, and Anxiety: Internal-External Control As a Moderator Variable," *Journal of Psychosomatic Research* 22 (1978): 205-8.
4. J. F. Igou and K. Caracci, "The Relationship between Locus of Control and Depression in Institutionalized Elderly" (paper presented at the meeting of the American Public Health Association, Washington, D.C., November 1985).
5. L. D. Egbert, et al., "Reduction of Postoperative Pain by Encouragement and Instruction of Patients," *New England Journal of Medicine* 270 (1964): 825-7.
6. Martin Seligman, *Learned Optimism* (New York: Knopf, 1991).
7. Daniel Goleman, *Emotional Intelligence* (New York: Bantam, 1995), 80-2.
8. Meyer Friedman and Ray Rosenman, *Type A Behavior and Your Heart* (New York: Knopf, 1974).

CHAPTER 5—WHY CONTROL FREAKS ACT THE WAY THEY DO

1. Amy Schwartz, *A Teeny Tiny Baby* (New York: Orchard Books, 1994).
2. Martin Seligman, *Helplessness* (New York: W. H. Freeman, 1992), 137.

CHAPTER 6—THE MEDDLING MANAGER

1. Rena Pasick, "Job Complexity, Worker Control, and Health" (paper presented at the annual meeting of the American Public Health Association, Washington, D.C., November 1985).
2. R. A. Karaseck, et al., "Job, Psychological Factors and Coronary Heart Disease," *Advances in Cardiology* 29 (1982): 62-7.
3. Steven Levy, "Working in Dilbert's World," *Newsweek* (August 12, 1996), 56.
4. Daniel Goleman, *Working with Emotional Intelligence* (New York: Bantam, 1998), 65.
5. S. M. Sales and J. House, "Job Dissatisfaction as a Possible Risk Factor in Coronary Heart Disease," *Journal of Chronic Diseases* 23 (1971): 861-73.

CHAPTER 7—THE COERCIVE COLLEAGUE

1. Ellen Langer and Susan Saegert, "Crowding and Cognitive Control," *Journal of Personality and Social Psychology* 35 (1977): 175-82.

2. William Glasser, *Control Theory: A New Explanation of How We Control Our Lives* (New York: Harper & Row, 1984), 163.

CHAPTER 8—THE SUPERVISING SPOUSE

1. Nancy Meyer, "Control Freaks Invade Market," *Weekly Home Furnishings Newspaper*, 20 June 1994, 52–3.
2. MSNBC Staff and Wire Report, 26 January 1999.

CHAPTER 9—THE PUSHY PARENT

1. This quotation and those that follow in this paragraph are taken from a 1748 article by J. Sulzer, "An Essay on the Education and Instruction of Children," quoted in Alice Miller, *For Your Own Good* (New York: Noonday Press, 1990), 11.
2. Elan Golomb, *Trapped in the Mirror: Adult Children of Narcissists in Their Struggle for Self* (New York: William Morrow, 1992).
3. Gustav Mahler, *Themes and Variations: An Autobiography*, trans. James Gulston (New York: Knopf, 1946), 81.
4. Heidi Resnick, "Prevalence of Civilian Trauma and Post-Traumatic Stress Disorder in a Representative National Sample of Women," *Journal of Consulting and Clinical Psychology* 61, no. 6 (December 1993): 984–91.
5. For further reading, see Charles Whitfield, *Boundaries and Relationships: Knowing, Protecting and Enjoying the Self* (Deerfield Beach, Fla.: Health Communications, 1993).
6. Moss Hart, as quoted in Robert Rains, *A Creative Brooding* (New York: Macmillan, 1977), 37–8.
7. Harold Bloomfield, *Making Peace with Your Parents* (New York: Ballantine Books, 1983).
8. Lewis B. Smedes, *The Art of Forgiving: When You Need to Forgive and Don't Know How* (Nashville: Moorings, 1996), 178.

CHAPTER 10—THE INVASIVE IN-LAW

1. W. Haws and B. Mallinckrodt, "Separation-Individuation from Family of Origin and Marital Adjustment of Recently Married Couples," *The American Journal of Family Therapy* 26 (1998): 293–306.

CHAPTER 11—THE TENACIOUS TEEN

1. Research reveals that more than 20 percent of adolescents experience excessive argumentativeness directed at either parent (more often with their mothers than with their fathers). See Robert Rains, *A Creative Brooding* (New York: Macmillan, 1977). Conflict between adolescents and their parents is different from conflict between peers. With parents the conflict is over both content (like how late to stay out) and over the process by which decisions are made. In other words, both the rules and the way the rules are made may become the subject of contro-

versy. The process usually relates to a perceived lack of freedom by the adolescent.

2. Haim G. Ginott, *Between Parent and Teenager* (New York: Avon, 1969), 43.
3. Erik H. Erikson, *Identity: Youth and Crisis* (New York: Norton, 1968), 28.
4. Huston Smith, *Chronicle of Higher Education* (June 20, 1997): 4.
5. Anne Roiphe, *Lovingkindness* (New York: Summit Books, 1987), 120.
6. Erikson, *Identity*.
7. Elizabeth Forsythe Haily, *A Woman of Independent Means* (New York: Viking Press, 1978), 198–9.

CHAPTER 13—SAFEGUARDS TO KEEP YOU FROM SPINNING OUT OF CONTROL

1. H. B. Beckman and R. M. Frankel, "The Effect of Physician Behavior on the Collection of Data," *Annals of Internal Medicine* 40 (1984): 101.

CHAPTER 14—REBUILDING YOUR RELATIONSHIPS

1. Tori DeAngelis, "A Nation of Hermits: The Loss of Community," *The American Psychological Association Monitor* (September 1995): 45–6.
2. Lewis B. Smedes, *Shame and Grace* (San Francisco: HarperCollins, 1993), 80.

CHAPTER 15—HOW TO TAKE CHARGE WITHOUT BEING A CONTROL FREAK

1. Henri Nouwen, *Sabbatical Journey* (New York: Crossroad Publishing, 1998), viii.

ABOUT THE AUTHOR

Dr. Les Parrott is founder and codirector (with his wife, Dr. Leslie Parrott) of the Center for Relationship Development on the campus of Seattle Pacific University (SPU), a groundbreaking program dedicated to teaching the basics of good relationships. Les is also a professor of psychology at SPU and the author of several best-selling books, including the award-winning *Saving Your Marriage Before It Starts, Becoming Soul Mates, A Good Friend,* and *High-Maintenance Relationships.*

Dr. Parrott is a sought-after speaker in corporate settings as well as in workshops and seminars throughout the country. He has written for a variety of magazines, and his work has been featured in *USA Today,* the *New York Times,* and the *Los Angeles Times.* Dr. Parrott's television appearances include *CNN, Good Morning America, The View,* and *Oprah.*

For information regarding speaking availability, seminar schedules, videos, books, and other resources, contact

Dr. Les Parrott
Center for Relationship Development
Seattle Pacific University
Seattle, WA 98119

Or, click on
www.RealRelationships.com